Hands-On English

Second Edition

Written by Fran Santoro Hamilton

Illustrated by Michael Hamilton

PORTICO
BOOKS

Portico Books, P. O. Box 6094, Chesterfield, MO 63006
Phone/Fax: 636-527-2822, 1-888-641-5353
www.GrammarAndMore.com • info@GrammarAndMore.com

Companion Products to *Hands-On English*
The Activity Book (practice pages)
Hands-On Sentences (card game)
Hands-On Icons (visual aids)

Learn more about these products and subscribe to **FREE** resources at
www.GrammarAndMore.com.
There is also an order form at the end of this book.

Copy Editing by Marnie Hauff

Printing and Binding by Corley Printing Company, St. Louis, MO

Previous edition copyrighted in 1998

First printing 2004

10 9 8 7 6 5 4 3 2 1

Printed in the United States of America

Publishers Cataloging in Publication Data

Hamilton, Fran Santoro
    Hands-on english / Fran Santoro Hamilton
        p.   cm.
    Includes index
    ISBN: 0-9664867-5-7
    1. English language—Grammar—Handbooks, manuals, etc.
    I. Title.
PE1097.H35 2004

428.24—dc22   PCN 2004091992

Dedicated
to all who grapple with the English language—
in work or in play

Author's Note on the Second Edition

What an incredible adventure the last six years have been—since the debut of *Hands-On English*! I've traveled tens of thousands of miles and have met thousands of people, some of whom I now count as dear friends. I've given dozens of interviews and presentations, written scores of newsletters, and fielded hundreds of questions. I've learned from everything—and everyone.

I thank everyone who has contributed to the success of *Hands-On English*. I appreciate your enthusiasm, your success stories, your endorsements, your suggestions. You encourage and inspire me.

Hands-On English is now in all fifty states and on six continents. It is used by gifted students and struggling students—and by adults who aren't formal students at all. *Hands-On English* is used in elementary schools, middle schools, high schools, home schools, colleges, adult education programs, ESL programs, offices, hospitals, prisons, libraries, no doubt in other places of which I'm not even aware.

When I first mentioned the possibility of a second edition, loyal customers said, "Don't change it! I like it just the way it is." I think—certainly *hope*—that those people will recognize the *Hands-On English* that they've come to love. As inventory ran low, however, I felt compelled to revisit *Hands-On English* with an editor's eye. Although many people have told me that *Hands-On English* is the clearest English book they've found, I discovered explanations that could be just a bit clearer. Now they are.

The second edition also has new material. Some topics have been expanded by a paragraph or two. The major additions, however, are in the Reading and Writing sections. The Reading section has new segments on words in context, denotation and connotation, finding the main idea, and decoding. The decoding segment focuses on dividing words into syllables and assigning the correct vowel sound. The Writing section has new segments on keeping an idea bank, developing paragraphs, writing compositions, and achieving conciseness.

There has never been a greater need for a clear, concise English book or for tools to help people communicate. To that end, I offer the second edition of *Hands-On English*.

Fran Santoro Hamilton

TABLE OF CONTENTS

TO THE USER OF THIS BOOK

Congratulations! You're lucky to be one of over 700,000,000 users of the English language.* About half of those people learn English as their first language. However, more people speak English as their *second* language than any other language on Earth.

English is spoken around the globe. It's used by pilots and air traffic controllers at international airports. Most printed and electronic communication, and most scientific and technical publications are written in English.

How did English come to be such an international language? Just as the United States is made up of people who have come from many nations, English includes words that have come from many languages. For centuries traders and warriors have carried their languages wherever they've gone. English was heavily influenced by Greek, Latin, French, and German. However, the roots of English go all the way back to ancient India!

When England began establishing colonies around the globe in the sixteenth century, her sailors and settlers took the English language with them. Some people they encountered learned English, and English, in turn, adopted many words from other languages.

See if you can match each English word in the list on the left below with its language of origin in the list on the right. (You can check your answers in a dictionary.)

aardvark	Afrikaans
alphabet	Arabic
camel	Cantonese
canyon	Egyptian
kindergarten	French
oasis	German
permission	Greek
shampoo	Hawaiian
ski	Hebrew
souvenir	Hindi
typhoon	Latin
ukulele	Norwegian
zero	Spanish

---

*Much of this information about English appeared in Richard Lederer's book *The Miracle of Language* (New York: Pocket Books, 1991), pages 19–32.

The preceding list contains only a small sample of the tens of thousands of colorful words that the English language has adopted from its colleagues.

Because English adopts words so freely, English has many more words than other languages have. Comprehensive English dictionaries list approximately half a million words. If technical, scientific, slang, and specialized words were added, the number would be about two million! Other major languages have fewer than 200,000 words; French, fewer than 100,000.

Because we have so many words from so many places, we often have many choices about how to say something. (A thesaurus will bring these choices to your fingertips.) Blue, for example, could be navy, turquoise, aquamarine, ultramarine, azure, cobalt, steel, or indigo.

The disadvantage of having words from so many languages is that English has many spellings that seem to be irregular. Consider, for example, how many different ways a particular sound, such as $\bar{o}$, can be spelled—or how many ways a particular spelling, such as *ough* can be pronounced.

I hope *Hands-On English* will provide you with quick access to the information you need (or want) about English. The table of contents will show you how the book is organized, and the index will help you find information on particular topics. Some sections of the book, such as the list of irregular verbs or the meanings of morphemes, would be good for you to study on your own.

I love to get letters, and I'd love to hear from *you*. Please let me know what you like about this book and how it helped you. I'd also like to know if you have suggestions for improving the book. Is there information you were looking for that you didn't find? Is there information that was unclear? Did you find an error?

I hope *Hands-On English* will help you to become a linguaphile or a verbivore. Those are terms that you probably won't find in a dictionary. If you find out what they mean, there's a good chance you've already become one!

Fran Hamilton
Portico Books
P.O. Box 6094
Chesterfield, MO 63006

GRAMMAR

Without being aware of it, you've been using grammar since you were a baby. When you first began to make sense of the things your parents were saying to you, you began to understand grammar. After hearing words such as *boys*, *girls*, *dogs*, and *cats*, you learned that an *s* at the end of some words makes them mean "more than one." You then applied this rule to form many other plurals. You probably even applied this rule to some words that form their plurals in other ways. You might have said *foots* instead of *feet*, for example, or *mouses* instead of *mice*. As you heard and read the English language over the years, you learned more about its rules and patterns.

Words are the building blocks of language. Although individual words have their own meanings, most communication uses words in combination. Word order is a very important part of grammar. How many different ideas can you communicate by combining the following words in different ways?

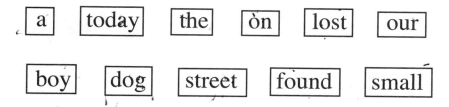

Using all of the words in each sentence, you should be able to make at least eight different sentences.

Becoming more familiar with the structure of language—with grammar—will make language easier for you to use, whether you're listening, talking, reading, writing, or just thinking.

1

PARTS OF SPEECH

Words can be classified into eight groups called **parts of speech.** Each part of speech has a <u>specific job</u> to do. A word's part of speech depends on the word's job in a particular sentence. Some words, such as *run*, can be one part of speech in one sentence and a different part of speech when they are working differently in another sentence.

NOUNS

A **noun** is a word that <u>names a person, a place, a thing, or an idea</u>.

    Persons: girl, uncle, cashier, chairperson, friend

    Places: park, school, city, fairgrounds, kitchen

    Things: building, stereo, puppy, week, hamburger

    Ideas: love, democracy, loyalty, truth, sadness

A word that ends in *-ness, -ment, -tion, -sion, -ion, -hood, -ism, -ist,* or *-ship* is usually a noun.

    happi**ness**   apart**ment**   atten**tion**   divi**sion**   un**ion**

    neighbor**hood**   patriot**ism**   art**ist**   friend**ship**

In this book we use a block to represent a noun. Nouns may be classified as **common nouns** or **proper nouns.** The nouns listed above are common nouns. They name persons, places, things, or ideas <u>in general</u>. A proper noun names a <u>particular</u> person, place, thing, or idea and <u>begins with a capital letter</u>. Examples of proper nouns are listed below.

    Persons: Uncle Joe, Mrs. Simmons, President Adams

    Places: Forest Park, Lincoln School, Clayton Road

    Things: Sears Tower, Lassie, Porsche, Big Mac

    Ideas: Christianity, Judaism, Islam, Hinduism

PRONOUNS

A **pronoun** is a word that's <u>used in place of a noun</u>. Because a pronoun is so similar to a noun, in this book we use a shaded block to represent a pronoun. You might think of a pronoun as a noun that's partly hidden by a veil. The meaning of the pronoun isn't completely clear until you know the noun the pronoun stands for.

Notice what happens when no pronouns are used:

> *Felipe and John worked on a social studies project together. Felipe and John worked at Felipe's house one day after school. Felipe's mom offered Felipe and John some cookies before Felipe and John began work.*

The paragraph sounds much smoother when pronouns are used:

> *Felipe and John worked on a social studies project together.* ***They*** *worked at Felipe's house one day after school.* ***His*** *mom offered* ***them*** *some cookies before* ***they*** *began work.*

The noun a pronoun stands for (called an **antecedent**) must always be clear. In the paragraph above, *his* stands for *Felipe's*, and *they* and *them* stand for *Felipe and John*. <u>The antecedent doesn't need to be in the same sentence with the pronoun.</u> Antecedents aren't clear in the following sentences.

> ***They*** *said* ***it*** *couldn't be done.* [*Who* said *what* couldn't be done? Meaning is unclear because no nouns are used.]

> *Kate loaned* ***her*** *ruler to Liz.* ***She*** *said* ***it*** *didn't have metric markings.* [Who said the ruler didn't have metric markings? Whether *she* refers to *Kate* or *Liz* is unclear.]

The chart on page 5 shows the most common pronouns, called **personal pronouns**. There are several other kinds of pronouns as well.

Indefinite pronouns, which are less specific than personal pronouns, are often used without an antecedent. Here are some examples. (Indefinite pronouns are discussed further on pages 33 and 34.)

all	both	each	someone
some	few	either	everyone
none	several	neither	anybody
	many	one	

Demonstrative pronouns demonstrate, or point out.

this	that	these	those

__That__ is the biggest pumpkin I've ever seen.

Interrogative pronouns are used to ask questions.

who	whom	what	which	whose

__Who__ called while I was out?

Reflexive pronouns are formed by adding *self* or *selves* to some personal pronouns.

myself	yourself	himself	herself	itself
ourselves	yourselves	themselves		

Notice that *hisself* and *theirselves* are not acceptable in standard usage.

A reflexive pronoun is used to carry action back to its antecedent or to emphasize its antecedent.

__Allison__ rewarded __herself__ with a ten-minute break.

__I myself__ have never been outside the United States.

Just as you can't have a reflection without an image, a reflexive pronoun shouldn't be used without an antecedent.

INCORRECT: *The gift is for Jo and myself.* [no antecedent]

CORRECT: *The gift is for Jo and me.*

4

PERSONAL PRONOUNS

	S I N G U L A R			P L U R A L		
	Subjective	Objective	Possessive	Subjective	Objective	Possessive
1st person	I	me	my, mine	we	us	our, ours
2nd person	you	you	your, yours	you	you	your, yours
3rd person	he she it	him her it	his her, hers its	they	them	their, theirs

First person refers to the speaker (or writer): *I am happy. We are happy.*
Second person refers to the person spoken *to: You are my best friend. You are all invited to the party.*
Third person refers to a person or thing spoken *about: She is going to the party. They are going to the party.*
(*She* and *they* are neither the persons speaking nor the persons spoken to.)

Only **subjective pronouns** should be used as the subject of a sentence or after a linking verb.
Only **objective pronouns** should be used as a direct object, an indirect object, or the object of a preposition.
Possessive pronouns are used to show ownership. In a sentence they work like adjectives, telling "which one."
Notice that no possessive pronoun contains an apostrophe, not even *its.*

ADJECTIVES

An **adjective** <u>modifies, or describes, a noun or pronoun.</u> It answers one of these questions: <u>What kind? Which one? How many?</u>

>   ***Three large red*** *trucks rolled down* ***that steep*** *hill.*

Large and *red* describe *trucks.* They tell "what kind" of trucks. *Three* also describes *trucks.* It tells "how many." *Steep* tells "what kind" of hill. *That* tells "which" hill. An adjective can change the picture created by a noun. Therefore, in this book we use a paintbrush (which can change the appearance of a block) to represent an adjective.

The great majority of adjectives tell *what kind.* Within this broad category are adjectives that tell *what color, what shape, what size,* etc. In addition to number words, adjectives that tell *how many* include words such as *some, several,* and *few.* The main adjectives that tell *which one* are *this, that, these,* and *those*—as well as the articles, discussed below.

To find which word an adjective describes, ask yourself which noun or pronoun it tells more about. You can also make a question using the adjective and the word *what*: TWO WHAT? LARGE WHAT? The answer to your question tells which word is being described—in this case, *trucks.*

Usually an adjective comes before the noun it describes, but sometimes it comes afterwards.

>   *The stamp is* ***old****.* [*Old* tells "what kind" of stamp.]

>   *The photo,* ***old*** *and* ***tattered****, was* ***precious****.*
>   [*Old, tattered,* and *precious* all describe *photo.*]

The most frequently used adjectives are *a, an,* and *the.* They're called **articles** or **noun markers**, and they tell "which one" or "how many." An article signals that a noun is coming. The only words that can occur between an article and its noun are other modifying words.

VERBS

A **verb** expresses <u>action</u> or a "<u>state of being</u>." We represent **action verbs** by a spring. Not all actions are observable.

>We **climbed** the stairs in the Statue of Liberty.

>We **hope** the weather will be nice for our camping trip.

A verb may consist of one word, as in the sentences above, or of several words. The main verb indicates the action that's taking place. The other words, called **helping verbs**, help to establish the **tense** of the verb, or the <u>time</u> when the action is occurring. <u>Helping verbs always come before the main verb.</u> However, sometimes other words come *between* the helping verb and the main verb.

>He **has read** fifteen books this year.

>You **should have recognized** your own picture.

>**Did** you **see** the moon tonight?

>I **could** not **find** him in the crowd.

The words listed below are often used as helping verbs. Those in the first column are forms of the verb *to be*, the most irregular of verbs. Helping verbs are often used in combination, as you saw above.

am	has	may
is	have	might
are	had	must
was	do	shall
were	does	should
be	did	could
been	can	would
being	will	

Words in the right-hand column are used *only* as helping verbs. However, the other verbs sometimes serve as the main verb of a sentence.

>She **is** a doctor.

>I **have** five silver bracelets from Mexico.

7

A **linking verb** doesn't involve action (even an action that isn't observable). Instead, it <u>links the subject of a sentence with a word in the predicate that helps to explain or describe it</u>. (A detailed discussion of subjects and predicates begins on page 16.) In this book we represent a linking verb with a chain.

> *He **is** a photographer.* [The linking verb *is* links the subject *he* with the noun *photographer*. *He* and *photographer* name the same person.]

> *They **were** angry.* [The linking verb *were* links the subject *they* with the adjective *angry*. *Angry* describes *they*.]

There are very few linking verbs. The linking verbs most often used are forms of the verb *to be*:

> am   is   are   was   were   been   be   being

The following verbs are often used as linking verbs. However, most of them can also be used as action verbs. Notice that the verbs in the first column have to do with sense impressions; those in the second column have to do with how something appears; those in the third column have to do with how something is or becomes.

taste	look	become
feel	appear	grow
smell	seem	remain
sound		stay

Linking verbs may be used with various helping verbs.

> *The injury **sounds** serious.* [The adjective *serious* describes the subject *injury*.]

> *The milk **will become** sour if you leave it on the table.* [The adjective *sour* describes the subject *milk*.]

> *Abby probably **would have remained** a sculptor if she had been able to earn a living at that job.* [The noun *sculptor* names the same thing as the subject *Abby*.]

Whether these words are linking verbs or action verbs depends upon how they are used. (For a more complete explanation, see page 28.)

> *Rob **tasted** the cake.* [*Taste* is an action verb telling what Rob did.]

> *The cake **tasted** sweet.* [The cake isn't doing the tasting. *Tasted* is a linking verb that links the subject *cake* with the adjective *sweet*. *Sweet* describes *cake*.]

> *Ashley **looked** at the volcanic rock.* [*Looked* is an action verb telling what Ashley did.]

> *Jeff **looked** pale.* [Jeff isn't doing the looking. The linking verb *looked* enables *pale* to describe *Jeff*.]

ADVERBS

Don't let the name fool you! <u>An adverb is not a verb.</u> An adverb <u>modifies — or describes — a verb, an adjective, or another adverb.</u> An adverb answers one of these questions: <u>How? When? Where? How much, or to what extent?</u> Because an adverb can modify so many words, answer so many questions, and appear so many places in a sentence, in this book we represent an adverb with a magic wand. A few of the thousands of adverbs are listed below.

How? slowly, carefully, quickly, well, loudly

When? soon, now, tomorrow, often, never, seldom

Where? here, there, up, down, outside, around

How much? very, too, so, really, completely, not

Adverbs that tell *when, where,* and *how* modify verbs. Often they can work equally well in several different places in a sentence. Adverbs that tell *how much* or *to what extent* modify adjectives or adverbs. They're placed in front of the words they modify.

9

Notice how adverbs are used in the following sentences.

> ***Today*** *Lauren is working **very slowly**.* [*Today* modifies the verb, telling "when" Lauren is working. *Slowly* also modifies the verb, telling "how" Lauren is working. *Very* modifies the adverb *slowly,* telling "to what extent" Lauren is working slowly.]

> *Lauren is working **very slowly today**.* [Notice that the sentence works as well with *today* at the end.]

You can find adverbs in a sentence by using the adverb's question words with the verb. For the sentences above, you'd ask, IS WORKING HOW? IS WORKING WHEN? IS WORKING WHERE?

The word *not* is an adverb. Often it's placed between a helping verb and a main verb. Even when it's part of a contraction (such as *isn't*), the *n't* part of the word is an adverb.

> *I will **not** allow you to go outside today.* [*Not* modifies the verb *will allow*, telling "to what extent."]

Most words that end in an *-ly* suffix are adverbs telling "how."

PREPOSITIONS

A **preposition** <u>shows the relationship between a noun or pronoun and another word in the sentence</u>. Thinking of single words that could appropriately complete the following sentence will supply you with a good list of prepositions.

> The rabbit ran _____ the yard.

Fewer than fifty words are commonly used as prepositions. Some of them aren't *always* prepositions, however; their part of speech depends upon how they're used. Becoming familiar with the prepositions on the next page will make it easier for you to analyze sentences.

aboard	below	inside	through
about	beneath	into	throughout
above	beside	like	to
across	between	near	toward
after	beyond	of	under
against	by	off	underneath
along	down	on	until
among	during	out	up
around	except	outside	upon
at	for	over	with
before	from	past	within
behind	in	since	without

Prepositions occur in phrases called **prepositional phrases**. A prepositional phrase <u>begins with a preposition</u> and <u>ends with the object of that preposition</u>. In this book we use a magnet to represent a preposition because a preposition always needs an object. The <u>noun or pronoun</u> that is the **object** of the preposition is labeled *OP* (object of preposition) to show its function. The only words that can occur between a preposition and its object are modifying words.

*The rabbit ran **into** the shady yard.*

From the list above, you can identify *into* as a preposition. To find the object of the preposition, ask yourself, INTO WHAT? The noun that answers that question is *yard. Shady* describes *yard.*

Prepositional phrases <u>work as either adjectives or adverbs</u>. To discover how a prepositional phrase is working, notice the kind of word it describes and the question it answers. Remember that adjectives modify nouns and pronouns, and tell *what kind, which one,* and *how many.* A prepositional phrase working as an adverb will modify a verb and will tell *how, when,* or *where.*

*The girl **with red hair** sang **at graduation**.*

With red hair tells "which" girl. Since it modifies a noun and tells "which one," the whole phrase is working as an adjective. *At graduation* tells "where" the girl sang. Since it modifies a verb and tells "where," the whole phrase is working as an adverb.

Two or more prepositional phrases can modify the same word.

*We jogged **around the lake at sunrise**.*

The phrases *around the lake* and *at sunrise* both modify the verb *jogged*. They're adverbial prepositional phrases, the first telling "where," the second telling "when."

Notice that one prepositional phrase can modify the object of another prepositional phrase.

*We met **at the southwest corner of the park**.*

At the southwest corner is an adverbial prepositional phrase that modifies the verb *met* and tells "where." *Of the park* is an adjectival prepositional phrase that modifies *corner* and tells "which one."

CONJUNCTIONS

A **conjunction** is a word that joins words or groups of words. The most common kind of conjunction is a **coordinating conjunction**. There are only seven coordinating conjunctions:

and   but   or   for   nor   so   yet

A coordinating conjunction can join individual words, phrases, or clauses. You must be sure, however, that you use a coordinating conjunction to join the same grammatical structures. In this book we use glue to represent coordinating conjunctions. You'd use a coordinating conjunction to join the same grammatical structures just as you might use glue to join two pieces of paper. The elements that are joined together make a **compound**.

*Our flag is red, white, **and** blue.* [Coordinating conjunction *and* joins adjectives in a series.]

*Fishing **and** gardening are two of my favorite outdoor activities.* [*And* joins *fishing* and *gardening*, making a compound subject. Subjects are discussed on page 16.]

12

*Our team played hard **but** lost the game.* [*But* joins two verb phrases, making a compound verb.]

*Our team played hard, **but** we lost the game.* [*But* joins two independent clauses; each could be a sentence by itself. See pages 17 and 18 for more about clauses.]

Notice the following INCORRECT example.

I like basketball, playing football, and to go swimming. [Because elements in the series don't have the same grammatical structure, we say they lack **parallelism**.]

REVISION: *I like basketball, football, and swimming.*

A **subordinating conjunction** joins an independent clause, which can stand alone, with a dependent clause, which cannot stand alone. In this book we use a screw to represent a subordinating conjunction. A subordinating conjunction joins two kinds of clauses as a screw might join metal to wood. Some of the common subordinating conjunctions include more than one word:

after	as soon as	since	whenever
although	because	so that	where
as	before	unless	wherever
as far as	even though	until	whether
as if	if	when	while

Notice that a clause introduced by a subordinating conjunction can come at either the beginning or the end of a sentence.

*The game was canceled **because** it rained.*

***Because** it rained, the game was canceled.*

A subordinating conjunction often relates the ideas in a sentence more precisely than a coordinating conjunction can relate them.

*Someone knocked on the door, **and** I opened it.*
[The coordinating conjunction *and* joins two independent clauses (equal grammatical structures). The sentence says only that two events happened, not how they're related.]

13

***When** someone knocked on the door, I opened it.*
[The subordinating conjunction shows that the ideas are related in time. We also see that opening the door is more important (because that idea is in the independent clause).]

Hearing a knock, I opened the door. [This sentence, which has only one clause and no conjunctions, gives even less importance to the knock.]

Many people misuse the phrase *as far as*. Since it is a subordinating conjunction, it should introduce a *clause*, not just a noun.

INCORRECT: *As far as my homework, I finished it.*

CORRECT: **As far as my <u>homework</u> <u>is concerned</u>,** *I finished it.*

CORRECT: *As for my homework, I finished it.* [*As for* works like a preposition. It needs only a noun or pronoun to be its object; it should not introduce a whole clause.]

The **relative pronouns** *who*, *whose*, *whom*, *which*, *that*, and *what* work like subordinating conjunctions in that they <u>introduce dependent clauses</u>. You should use *who*, *whose*, and *whom* to refer to people. You should use *that* and *which* to refer to animals or things.

*The man **who** lives next door to us is an author.*
[The dependent clause *who lives next door to us* interrupts the independent clause *The man is an author.*]

*Jupiter, **which** is the largest planet in the solar system, has twelve moons.* [The dependent clause *which is the largest planet in the solar system* interrupts the independent clause *Jupiter has twelve moons.*]

*Dad returned the books **that** I had read.* [The dependent clause *that I had read* follows the independent clause *Dad returned the books.*]

Sometimes a relative pronoun is only implied rather than stated.

Dad returned the books I had read. [**That** from the previous example has been omitted. However, the two clauses have the same relationship, and the sentence has the same meaning.]

Correlative conjunctions are used in pairs.

both . . . and   either . . . or
not only . . . but also   neither . . . nor

You must be sure that the same kind of grammatical construction (word, phrase, or clause) follows each item in the pair. This is another example of parallelism. Study the following examples.

INCORRECT: *We will either* **go to Colorado** *or* **Virginia**. [*Either* is followed by a verb phrase; however, its partner, *or*, is followed by a proper noun.]

CORRECT: *We will go either* **to Colorado** *or* **to Virginia**. [Both *either* and *or* are followed by prepositional phrases.]

CORRECT: *We will go to either* **Colorado** *or* **Virginia**. [Both *either* and *or* are followed by nouns.]

INTERJECTIONS

An **interjection** has <u>no grammatical relationship to the rest of the sentence</u>. In keeping with the meaning of its word parts (*ject* meaning "throw" and *inter* meaning "between or among"), it's just "thrown into" the sentence. We use a triangular pyramid (a tetrahedron) to represent an interjection. When an interjection expresses strong feeling, it's followed by an exclamation point. In other situations it's followed by a comma.

Ouch! I cut my finger.

Wow! We won!

Oh, I wondered where that pen was.

SENTENCES

Except in informal communication, words are generally arranged in **sentences**. A sentence is a group of words containing a subject and a predicate, and expressing a complete thought. Knowing about sentences can help you to understand complicated sentences that you hear or read. It can also help you to use more mature sentences in your speech and writing.

SUBJECTS AND PREDICATES

The **subject** of a sentence must contain a noun or a pronoun. It names something. The **predicate** of a sentence contains a verb. It tells what the subject does.

> *Dogs bark.*

In the example above, the subject is *dogs*; the predicate, or verb, is *bark*. Both the subject part of a sentence and the predicate part of a sentence may include modifying words and phrases.

> ***The** dogs **in the next yard** bark **loudly at night**.*

Finding Subjects and Predicates. In analyzing a sentence, it's usually easiest to find the verb, or action word, first. Ask yourself what is happening in the sentence. In the example above, the verb is *bark*.

To find the simple subject of the sentence, ask yourself, WHO BARK? The answer, of course, is *dogs*. The **simple subject** and **simple predicate** (or verb) have words describing them. *Dogs* and all of the words and phrases describing it make up the **complete subject**; *bark* and all of the words and phrases describing it make up the **complete predicate**.

In the example on the next page, the simple subject is underlined once, and the simple predicate is underlined twice. A vertical line separates the complete subject from the complete predicate. (Many grammar books show subjects and predicates by marking sentences like this.)

16

*The **dogs** in the next yard | **bark** loudly at night.*

Sometimes it's not easy to find the verb in a sentence. Perhaps the verb is a linking verb (discussed on pages 8 and 9). Here are some simple ways you can check a word to see if it's a verb.

1. Is the word a linking verb or another word that is always a verb? (*is, am, are, was, were, has, have, had, should, could, would*)

2. Does the word have various forms that could be used to indicate something happening in the past, present, or future? (*walk, walked, will walk; sing, sang, sung*)

3. Can you use the word with a pronoun to indicate an action or make a statement? (*I walk; she walks; he is; they are; we sing*)

4. Can you add an *-ed* or *-ing* suffix to the word? (*be-ing, visit-ed, dream-ing*)

Not every test will work for every verb, but if the word you're testing is indeed a verb, usually at least one of the tests will work.

CLAUSES

A **clause** is a group of words containing a subject and a predicate. As you might guess, some clauses—those that express a complete thought—can stand alone as complete sentences. They're called **independent clauses**. In this book we use a block and a spring to represent an independent clause. The subject is a noun or pronoun, and the predicate is a verb. (Later we'll look at independent clauses that have linking verbs.) The example sentences used so far in this Sentences section are independent clauses with action verbs.

> *The **plants received** plenty of sunlight and water.*
> [This clause includes a subject and a verb, and expresses a complete thought. Therefore, it can stand alone as a complete sentence. Notice that the symbols show only the basic structure of the sentence, not every word.]

17

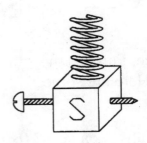

Some clauses contain a subject and verb but don't express a complete thought. They're called **dependent clauses** (or **subordinate clauses**) because they <u>can't stand alone as complete sentences</u>. Our symbol for a dependent clause includes a block and spring (just like the independent clause). A screw has been added because the dependent clause also includes a subordinating conjunction. Just as a dependent clause doesn't make a complete sentence, this symbol looks incomplete because the screw isn't attaching the block to anything.

> *When the **plants** **received** plenty of sunlight and water.*
> [This group of words is a clause because it contains a subject and a verb. It does not express a complete thought, however. We wonder, *When the plants received plenty of sunlight and water,* WHAT HAPPENED? Because there are a subject and a verb but the thought is incomplete, this is a dependent clause.]

You'll soon see how dependent and independent clauses can be combined to make different kinds of sentences.

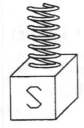

SIMPLE SENTENCES

A **simple sentence** has just <u>one independent clause</u> (one group of words containing a subject and a predicate, and expressing a complete thought).

> *<u>Dogs</u> <u>bark</u>.*

> *The **dogs** in the next yard **bark** loudly at night.*

Notice that simple sentences might not be short. They may have many modifiers. They're called *simple* because they have just one clause.

18

COMPOUND SENTENCES

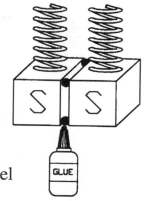

A sentence consisting of <u>two or more independent clauses</u> is called a **compound sentence**. In our model for a compound sentence you see two symbols for independent clauses joined by glue, which represents a coordinating conjunction.

In the examples below, each independent clause is enclosed in brackets. Notice that the independent clauses can be joined by a comma plus a coordinating conjunction, or by a semicolon.

[*__Josh__ __plays__ soccer*]**,** *and* [*__Jenny__ __plays__ golf.*]

[*In May __we__ __go__ to Michigan*]**;** [*in June __we__ __go__ to Texas.*]

COMPOUND SUBJECTS AND VERBS

Subjects joined by a coordinating conjunction make a compound subject. Verbs joined by a coordinating conjunction make a compound verb (or compound predicate). A sentence with a compound subject or a compound verb is a simple, not a compound, sentence. It contains only one independent clause. In the sentences that follow, vertical lines separate the complete subject from the complete predicate. <u>Notice that a comma is not used between the two parts of a compound subject or compound verb.</u>

__Rachel__ and __Akiko__ | *__are going__ to the zoo.*

The __girls__ | *__went__ to the zoo and __saw__ the seals.*

The __men__ and __women__ | *__sat__ still and __listened__ quietly.*

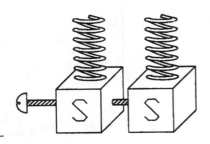

COMPLEX SENTENCES

A **complex sentence** has <u>an independent clause and a dependent clause</u>. You see both kinds of clauses in our model. First let's look at some dependent clauses.

*Because **we were** late*. [The dependent clause is introduced by a subordinating conjunction. See page 13 for a list of subordinating conjunctions.]

Which was broken. [The dependent clause is introduced by a relative pronoun. Other relative pronouns are *who*, *whom*, *whose*, *that*, and *what*.]

In order to make each of the preceding examples a complete sentence, an entire independent clause must be added. Notice that each independent clause could be a sentence by itself.

Dependent   **Independent**
[*Because **we were** late,*] [***we missed*** *our plane*.]

Independent   **Dependent**
[***This is*** *the vase*] [***that was broken***.]

Notice that a dependent clause can interrupt an independent clause:

[***that was broken***]
[*The **vase**   **is fixed** now*.]

The independent clause in the sentence above is *The vase is fixed now*.

COMPOUND–COMPLEX

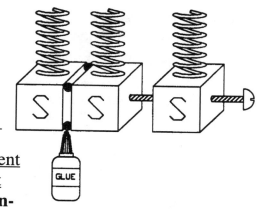

A sentence with <u>at least one dependent clause and two or more independent clauses</u> is a **compound–complex sentence**. The model has three clauses—two joined by a coordinating conjunction and the other attached with a subordinating conjunction.

<u>*We*</u> <u>*were planning*</u> *a cruise,*　　　[independent clause]

but <u>*we*</u> <u>*kept*</u> *it secret*　　　[independent clause]

until <u>*we*</u> <u>*bought*</u> *our tickets.*　　　[dependent clause]

The dependent clause can appear anywhere in this kind of sentence.

SENTENCE FRAGMENTS

There are three requirements for a complete sentence: The sentence must (1) contain a subject, (2) contain a predicate, and (3) express a complete thought. If a "sentence" fails to do any one of these things, it is an <u>incomplete sentence</u>, or a **sentence fragment**. Most people use many sentence fragments in informal conversation. However, you should avoid fragments in writing and in formal speech. Here are some common kinds of sentence fragments.

1. *The boy behind me.* This is a subject only; it has no predicate. It names someone but doesn't tell what the person did.

2. *Dropped a tack.* This is a predicate only; it has no subject. It tells what happened but doesn't tell who performed the action. (See page 24 for information about imperative sentences, which might at first appear to lack a subject. Imperative sentences have an implied subject, however. They are not fragments.)

21

3. *Missing the street sign.* This is a participial phrase containing neither a subject nor a predicate. <u>A verb ending in *-ing* can't be the only verb in a sentence</u>; it needs a helping verb: *She **is** missing the street sign.* Often a participial phrase introduces the independent clause: *Missing the street sign, **she drove** two blocks too far.*

4. *With a chip on his shoulder.* This is a pair of prepositional phrases. It contains neither a subject nor a predicate. Notice how both a subject and a predicate must be added to make a complete sentence: ***He walks** with a chip on his shoulder.*

5. *When she reached the finish line.* This may be the most common type of sentence fragment. After all, it meets two of the three tests for a complete sentence: It contains a subject (*she*) and a verb (*reached*). However, the word *when* makes this a dependent, rather than an independent, clause. It can't stand alone because it doesn't express a complete thought. It leaves a question in your mind: *When she reached the finish line*, WHAT HAPPENED? To complete the sentence, an entire independent clause must be added: *When <u>she reached</u> the finish line, **she collapsed** on the ground.*

6. *Which I left at home.* This is a dependent clause introduced by a relative pronoun; it must be in the same sentence as the word the pronoun stands for. Notice that an independent clause must be added to complete the sentence: ***I need** my kit, which <u>I left</u> at home.*

To turn a fragment into a complete sentence, you generally need to add a word, a phrase, or an independent clause.

RUN-ON SENTENCES

A **run-on sentence** is the opposite of a fragment. It consists of <u>two or more independent clauses without proper punctuation</u>. There are three ways to correctly punctuate independent clauses:

1. *We worked all day. We played all evening.* [Clauses are punctuated as separate sentences.]

2. *We worked all day; we played all evening.* [Clauses are separated with a semicolon; a lowercase letter begins the second clause.]

22

3. *We worked all day, and we played all evening.* [Clauses are separated with a comma plus a coordinating conjunction.]

In each of the following INCORRECT examples, clauses are not properly separated, and a run-on sentence results.

> *We worked all day we played all evening.*
>
> *We worked all day, we played all evening.*
>
> *We worked all day, then we played all evening.*
>
> *We worked all day, however we played all evening.*

Remember that there are only seven coordinating conjunctions (words that can join independent clauses): *and, but, or, for, nor, so, yet.*

Then, however, and *therefore* require stronger punctuation.

Run-ons often occur when the second clause begins with a pronoun that refers to a noun in the first clause. Although the pronoun reference must be clear, the noun and pronoun needn't be in the same sentence.

> INCORRECT: *We were all excited about the game, it was the league championship.*

This run-on should be corrected by making separate sentences or by using a semicolon. The third method (using a comma plus a coordinating conjunction) doesn't work well in this case.

> CORRECT: *We were all excited about the game. It was the league championship.*
>
> CORRECT: *We were all excited about the game; it was the league championship.*

<u>Often a run-on sentence can best be fixed by relating the two ideas in some other way—by making one idea more important than the other</u>:

> *We were all excited about the game because it was the league championship.*

23

We were all excited about the game, the league championship.

We were all excited about the game to determine the league champion.

We were all excited about the league championship game.

PURPOSES OF SENTENCES

Sentences can be classified according to one of four purposes. A **declarative** sentence <u>makes a statement</u>.

It is snowing outside.

Many people think Abe Lincoln was a great President.

An **interrogative** sentence <u>asks a question</u>.

Where were you when the lights went out?

An **imperative** sentence <u>makes a request or command</u>. The subject of an imperative sentence usually is not stated in the sentence. It is "understood" to be the person hearing or reading the sentence. Therefore, the subject of an imperative sentence is said to be "understood you" or "implied you." Because the subject is not stated, it's possible to have a complete imperative sentence with only one word.

Watch.

Please close the door.

Sit, Fido.

An **exclamatory** sentence <u>shows strong feeling</u>. Declarative or imperative sentences might be exclamatory.

I won the election! [declarative]

Leave me alone! [imperative]

SENTENCE PATTERNS

Sentences follow one of five basic sentence patterns. Being able to identify the basic structure of a long, complicated sentence can help you understand the sentence's meaning. Models using our symbols for the parts of speech show the *essential* elements of these sentences. The sentences may contain many other words, however.

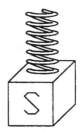

SUBJECT—VERB

The simplest of the five basic patterns is Subject–Verb (S–V). This pattern is used to tell that someone or something does something. In addition to the simple subject and action verb, the sentence may contain helping verbs, adjectives, adverbs, and prepositional phrases.

> **S**   **V**
> *Birds chirp.*

>   **S**
> *Two yellow birds on the branches of the pine tree*

>   **V**
> *have been chirping merrily this sunny morning.*

As you can see, a S–V sentence isn't necessarily short. However, it won't include any of the elements named in the other patterns.

SUBJECT—LINKING VERB—PREDICATE NOUN

The second pattern consists of a subject, a linking verb, and a **predicate noun** (S–LV–PN). This pattern is used to tell who someone is or what something is. (Reviewing the list of linking verbs on page 8 might help you identify this pattern.) <u>Remember that the noun following a linking verb must name</u>

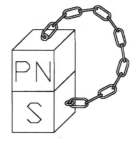

the same thing the subject names. It's called a predicate noun because it's in the predicate part of the sentence. S–LV–PN sentences may also contain descriptive words and phrases.

S LV PN
He is my father. [*He* and *father* name the same person.]

S   **LV**
The tall man in the corner by the fireplace is my loving,

P N
generous father. [*Man* and *father* name the same person.]

A predicate noun will never be part of a prepositional phrase.

S LV PN prep. obj.
Second prize is a check for twenty dollars.
[At first you might think that *dollars* is the predicate noun because it names the same thing as *prize*. It can't be a predicate noun though because it's in a prepositional phrase.]

SUBJECT—LINKING VERB—PREDICATE ADJECTIVE

The third pattern (S–LV–PA) consists of a subject, a linking verb, and a predicate adjective. It is used to describe someone or something. The **predicate adjective**, so named because it's part of the predicate, must describe the subject of the sentence. Notice how this is shown in our model for this sentence pattern: The paintbrush (adjective) is joined to the block (noun) by a chain (linking verb) and is painting (or modifying) it. S–LV–PA sentences may contain other descriptive words and phrases.

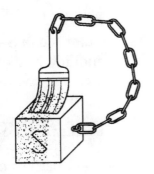

S LV PA
She is tall. [*Tall* describes *she*.]

S
The chocolate birthday cake on the dining room table

LV   **PA**
looks indescribably delicious. [*Delicious* describes *cake*.]

Notice the difference in structure between these two sentences.

S   **LV**   **PA**
Football   *is*   *rough.*

S   **LV**   **PN**
Football   *is*   *a*   *rough*   *sport.*

Although the two sentences mean about the same thing, they show different basic patterns. In the first sentence, the adjective *rough* describes the subject *football*; it's a predicate adjective. In the second sentence, the adjective *rough* describes the predicate noun *sport*, which names the same thing as the subject *football*. <u>One verb would never have both a predicate noun and a predicate adjective.</u>

Notice that sentence elements may be compound:

S   **S** **LV** **PN**
Ryan and Sean are brothers.

S **LV**   **PN**   **PN**
She   *is*   *my*   *neighbor*   *and*   *my*   *friend.*

S   **S** **LV** **PA**   **PA**
The   *boys*   *and*   *girls*   *were*   *hot*   *and*   *tired.*

S   **S** **LV** **PN**   **PN**
Erin and Megan are secretary and treasurer respectively.
[The word *respectively* indicates that words are to be paired in the order named. In this case, Erin is the secretary, and Megan is the treasurer.]

27

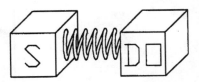 The fourth sentence pattern (S–V–DO) includes a subject, an action verb, and a **direct object**, usually in this order. This pattern is used to tell that someone or something (S) is doing something (V) to someone or something else (DO). The model shows that this pattern uses an action verb rather than a linking verb.

To find the direct object in a sentence, form a question by asking, SUBJECT VERB WHAT? Notice how this works in the following sentences.

    S V   DO

She tasted the delicious-looking cake on the dining room table. [SHE TASTED WHAT? *cake*]

              S   V   DO

A small boy in a green jacket took my radio from the porch. [BOY TOOK WHAT? *radio*]

    S   V   DO   DO

Becky <u>could have found</u> Dave and me at the mall.
[BECKY COULD HAVE FOUND WHOM? *Dave and me*]

Direct Object or Predicate Noun? Predicate nouns and predicate adjectives could also answer the question SUBJECT VERB WHAT? However, you'll be able to distinguish them from direct objects if you keep these three points in mind.

1. Predicate nouns and predicate adjectives follow *linking* verbs; direct objects follow *action* verbs. Be familiar with the list of linking verbs on page 8.

2. Subjects of action verbs perform action; subjects of linking verbs don't perform action.

3. Predicate nouns or predicate adjectives must name or describe the subject of the sentence. Direct objects indicate who or what is *receiving the action of the subject*; they don't rename the subject.

        S   V   DO
Emily decorated the cake. [Emily is doing the decorating;
Emily and *cake* do not name the same thing.]

        S   LV   PN
Emily is a cake decorator. [Emily is not performing action; *Emily* and *decorator* name the same person.]

SUBJECT–VERB–INDIRECT OBJECT–DIRECT OBJECT

The fifth pattern (S–V–IO–DO) consists
of a subject, an action verb, an **indirect
object**, and a direct object. The elements
are normally in this order in English. In
addition to the information presented in
the S–V–DO sentence, this pattern also
tells *to whom* or *for whom* the action is
being done. Although, as we've seen, a
sentence can include a direct object with-
out an indirect object (S–V–DO), <u>a sentence can't include an indirect
object without also including a direct object.</u>

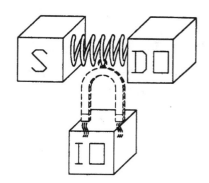

The following sequence shows the questions to ask in analyzing a sentence. First find the verb.

            V
I bought my mother a present. [To find the subject, ask
WHO BOUGHT?]

S   V
I bought my mother a present. [To find the direct object,
ask I BOUGHT WHAT?]

S   V   DO
I bought my mother a present. [To find the indirect object, ask I BOUGHT A PRESENT FOR WHOM?]

S   V   IO   DO
I bought my mother a present.

Here are more examples of the S–V–IO–DO pattern.

> **S**   **V**   **IO**   **DO**
> *The audience gave the cast a standing ovation.*

> **S**   **V**   **IO**   **DO**
> *The teacher gave us a big assignment in science.*

Indirect Object or Object of a Preposition? An indirect object is very much like a prepositional phrase with the preposition omitted. Notice that the questions used to locate indirect objects include prepositions: *To* whom? *For* whom? That's why our model for the S–V–IO–DO sentence shows the indirect object suspended from the verb by an "invisible" preposition. The preposition is only implied, making an indirect object.

Compare the following pairs of sentences. The first of each pair contains a prepositional phrase, and the second contains an indirect object. The sentences in each pair have about the same meaning.

> **S**   **V**   **DO** **prep. obj.**
> *She handed a ticket to me.*

> **S**   **V**   **IO**   **DO**
> *She handed me a ticket.*

> **S**   **V**   **DO** **prep. obj.**
> *I* <u>*will buy*</u> *a soda for you.*

> **S**   **V**   **IO**   **DO**
> *I* <u>*will buy*</u> *you a soda.*

USAGE

Usage involves the way language is used in speaking or writing. Many things affect a person's usage. For example, a three-year-old child uses language differently from the way an adult uses it. People in New England, the South, and the Midwest may choose different words and use different pronunciations. Most people use English differently in different situations. Language used during a presentation in school or on the job is likely to be different from language used in informal situations with family or friends.

This section will help you know usage that is acceptable when you are speaking to an educated audience. Questions about usage are most likely to involve verbs, pronouns, or modifiers (adjectives or adverbs).

USING VERBS

Correct verb usage involves having the verb agree in number with its subject. Correct verb usage also involves choosing the correct form of an irregular verb and knowing which of two similar verbs is appropriate in a given situation.

SUBJECT–VERB AGREEMENT

For most sentences that you speak or write, subject and verb agreement won't be a problem. However, understanding the rules of subject–verb agreement will guide you through tricky situations.

1. Each noun or pronoun is either singular or plural. It is **singular** if it names <u>one</u> thing. It is **plural** if it names <u>more than one</u> thing. Notice the singular and plural forms of the following words.

Singular	book	dish	sky	child	I
Plural	books	dishes	skies	children	we

2. The subject and verb of a sentence must agree in number. That means that if the subject is singular, the verb must also be singular; if the subject is plural, the verb must also be plural. <u>Notice that an -s ending on a third-person verb indicates the *singular* form.</u>

   *The **bee buzzes**.* [singular subject and singular verb]

   *The **bees buzz**.*   [plural subject and plural verb]

3. When a sentence contains a verb phrase, the *helping verb* is the part that must agree with the subject.

   *For thirty minutes <u>he</u> **<u>has</u> <u>been</u> <u>waiting</u>** for the bus.*
   [singular subject and verb *has*]

   *For half an hour <u>they</u> **<u>have</u> <u>been</u> <u>waiting</u>** for the bus.*
   [plural subject and verb *have*]

4. Remember that it is the *subject* that must agree in number with the verb. Prepositional phrases that come between the subject and the verb don't affect verb choice. Remember that a subject can never be in a prepositional phrase.

   *A **network** of nerves **carries** messages through the body.*

   The sentence may sound awkward or wrong with the singular verb *carries* right after the plural noun *nerves*. However, the subject of the sentence—the word that must agree with the verb—is *network*. Both the subject and the verb are singular.

5. These indefinite pronouns are *singular* and take singular verbs.

one	anyone	no one
each	anybody	nobody
either	everyone	someone
neither	everybody	somebody

   Everybody or *everyone* may logically seem plural. However, looking at the second word in these compounds (the singular *body* and *one*) may help you remember that these pronouns are singular.

   ***Everyone** likes the new teacher.* [singular subject and verb]

   ***Each** of the students **has** a sack lunch.* [singular]

6. These indefinite pronouns are *plural* and require a plural verb.

both	few	many	several

   ***Few** of my friends **like** peas.* [plural subject and verb]

7. The following indefinite pronouns may be either singular or plural, depending on the sense of the sentence.

all	any	most	none	some

   If the pronoun refers to one person or thing, it's singular and takes a singular verb. If the pronoun refers to more than one person or thing, it's plural and requires a plural verb.

__All__ of our attention __was focused__ on the movie. [The pronoun *all* refers to *attention*, which is singular. It requires the singular helping verb *was*.]

__All__ of the students __were awarded__ a prize. [The pronoun *all* refers to *students*, which is plural. It requires the plural helping verb *were*.]

__Some__ of the excitement of being on vacation __was lost__ after the first three days. [*Some* refers to *excitement*, which is singular.]

__Some__ of the students __prefer__ Sarah for class president; others prefer Andy. [*Some* refers to *students*, which is plural.]

To indicate whether they are singular or plural, the subjects of the two preceding sentences may be diagramed as shown below.

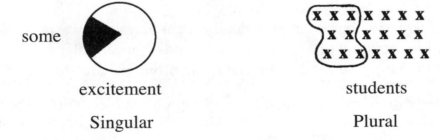

some

              excitement   students

               Singular   Plural

8. Subjects joined by *and* take a plural verb. [1 + 1 = 2]

   A __knife__ and a __fork__ __are used__ for cutting and eating meat. [plural]

Sometimes a plural idea is expressed with words such as *with*, *plus*, or *as well as*. These words are prepositions and do *not* compound the subject.

   A good night's __sleep__, __as well as__ regular exercise, __is__ important for good health. [singular]

If a plural subject is meant, this kind of sentence may be written more effectively as a compound.

34

*A good night's <u>sleep</u> **and** regular <u>exercise</u> <u>are</u> important for good health.* [plural]

9. Singular subjects joined by *or* or *nor* take a singular verb. **[1 or 1 = 1]**

   *A <u>**dog**</u> or a <u>**cat**</u> <u>**makes**</u> a good pet.* [singular]

   *Neither <u>**Mom**</u> nor <u>**Dad**</u> <u>**likes**</u> to cook.* [singular]

10. When a singular subject and a plural subject are joined by *or* or *nor*, the verb agrees with the nearer subject to make the sentence sound better.

    *Neither the <u>**teacher**</u> nor the <u>**students**</u> <u>**understand**</u> the speaker.* [plural verb to agree with *students*]

    *Neither the <u>**students**</u> nor the <u>**teacher**</u> <u>**understands**</u> the speaker.* [singular verb to agree with *teacher*]

11. Collective nouns (nouns that are singular in form but name a group of people or things) may be either singular or plural, depending on the meaning of the sentence. Here are examples of collective nouns.

audience	committee	flock	majority
band	crew	group	orchestra
chorus	crowd	herd	team
class	family	jury	troop

*The <u>**jury**</u> <u>**has reached**</u> a verdict.* [*Jury* is singular because the verdict belongs to the jury as a unit.]

*The **jury** **are arguing** about the defendant's guilt.* [*Jury* is plural because members are considered individually; the subject must be plural in order for arguing to occur.]

Some correct sentences with collective nouns (such as the previous example) might sound awkward to you. Usually there is a way to revise a sentence so that it is graceful as well as correct.

*The **jurors** **are arguing** about the defendant's guilt.* [The collective noun has been replaced with a plural noun.]

12. Words stating amounts are usually singular.

*Seventy-five **cents** **is** not enough money for lunch.* [A singular verb is used because *seventy-five cents* is being considered as one amount, not as separate cents.]

13. The title of a book, organization, or country—even when plural in form—usually takes a singular verb. After all, the country, book, etc. is being considered as *one* thing.

*The **United States** **is** my homeland.* [singular]

***The Twenty-One Balloons** **is** an imaginative book.* [singular]

14. Some nouns, although they end in *s*, are actually singular and take a singular verb. These words are examples.

civics	mathematics	mumps	physics
economics	measles	news	rickets

*The **news is** on at 6:00.* [singular]

__Physics includes__ the study of light, heat, sound, mechanics, and electricity. [singular]

15. Remember that *there* and *here* can never be subjects. If a sentence begins with one of these words, locate the subject carefully so that the verb will agree with it in number. Remember, too, that *there's* and *here's* (contractions for *there is* and *here is*) are singular. Don't use one of these contractions if your subject is plural.

*There **are** several **reasons** to fasten your seat belt.* [plural]

*Here **are** your **ruler**, **compass**, and **protractor**.* [plural]

PRINCIPAL PARTS OF VERBS

The verb is the part of the sentence that indicates *when* the action of the sentence takes place—whether in the past, the present, or the future. This feature of a verb is called **tense**. You should use the same tense to tell about things that happened in the same time frame. You shouldn't shift back and forth between past and present tenses, for example. Notice these short summaries of *The Twenty-One Balloons*.

INCONSISTENT:

*William Waterman Sherman, a retired professor, **left** San Francisco on August 15, 1883. He **hoped** to be the first person to cross the Pacific Ocean in a hot-air balloon. Instead, he **has** a marvelous adventure on the island of Krakatoa, in Indonesia.*

CONSISTENT:

*William Waterman Sherman, a retired professor, **left** San Francisco on August 15, 1883. He **hoped** to be the first person to cross the Pacific Ocean in a hot-air balloon. Instead, he **had** a marvelous adventure on the island of Krakatoa, in Indonesia.* [past tense]

37

CONSISTENT:

*William Waterman Sherman, a retired professor, **leaves** San Francisco on August 15, 1883. He **hopes** to be the first person to cross the Pacific Ocean in a hot-air balloon. Instead, he **has** a marvelous adventure on the island of Krakatoa, in Indonesia.* [present tense, sometimes used for summaries]

Tenses are formed from the four principal parts of each verb.

The **base word** is the simplest form of the verb. It's the form that's listed as an entry word in the dictionary. For most verbs, the **infinitive** and the **present** tense (except third person singular) are identical to the base word. The base word is used as the main verb in a present-tense sentence or in combination with helping verbs *do, does, did, may, might, must, can, could, shall, should, will,* and *would.* Often the infinitive is preceded by the word *to.* <u>An infinitive, which has no tense, can never be the main verb of a sentence.</u>

> *They **check** the temperature every morning.* [present]
>
> *She **will check** the depth of the water before diving.* [helping verb + base word = future tense]
>
> *Don't forget **to check** the roast at 6:00.* [The main verb is *do forget*; *to check* is an infinitive.]

The **past** is the second principal part of the verb. It's used to tell about something that already happened. The past form is used without a helping verb.

> *We **checked** our homework in class.*

The **past participle** is the third principal part of the verb. It's used with the helping verb *have, has,* or *had* to tell about something that happened in the past, often something that continued for a while.

> *She **has** already **checked** her coat.*
>
> *We **have checked** the temperature every day this week.*

38

The **present participle** is the fourth principal part of the verb. It has an *-ing* ending. A present participle by itself isn't enough to be the whole verb in a sentence. It must always be used with a helping verb that's some form of the verb *to be*.

> *Kendra **is checking** three books out of the library.*

> ***Checking** his swing.* [sentence fragment]

Regular verbs form their second and third principal parts simply by adding *-ed* to the base word. (For more information about spelling changes that may be needed as the suffix is added, see pages 93–95.)

Base Word	Past	Past Participle	Present Participle
look	looked	(have) looked	looking
save	saved	(have) saved	saving
grab	grabbed	(have) grabbed	grabbing
try	tried	(have) tried	trying

Irregular verbs form their second and third principal parts in more unusual ways, leading to most of the problems in verb usage. Tricky as these verbs are, you probably already use most of them correctly. If you memorize the principal parts of those that give you trouble, and if you understand how to form various tenses, you'll improve verb use.

Two lists of irregular verbs follow. The first is arranged alphabetically so that you can quickly check the principal parts of a particular verb. The second list groups verbs that follow a similar pattern in forming their principal parts. These words might be easier for you to remember if you study them together.

The English language is a living entity that is constantly changing. Some verbs show alternative forms for their past and/or past participle. An effort has been made to list the preferred form first. However, authorities may disagree on this.

The dictionary is another source for finding principal parts of verbs. Unless a verb is regular, a dictionary will show its principal parts. They usually appear in boldface type near the beginning of the entry.

PRINCIPAL PARTS OF IRREGULAR VERBS
(ALPHABETICAL LIST)

Base Word	Past	Past Participle	Present Participle
beat	beat	(have) beaten	beating
become	became	(have) become	becoming
begin	began	(have) begun	beginning
bet	bet	(have) bet	betting
bite	bit	(have) bitten *or* (have) bit	biting
blow	blew	(have) blown	blowing
break	broke	(have) broken	breaking
bring	brought	(have) brought	bringing
catch	caught	(have) caught	catching
choose	chose	(have) chosen	choosing
come	came	(have) come	coming
cost	cost	(have) cost	costing
cut	cut	(have) cut	cutting
do	did	(have) done	doing
draw	drew	(have) drawn	drawing
drink	drank	(have) drunk	drinking
drive	drove	(have) driven	driving
drown	drowned	(have) drowned	drowning
eat	ate	(have) eaten	eating
fall	fell	(have) fallen	falling
fly	flew*	(have) flown	flying
freeze	froze	(have) frozen	freezing
get	got	(have) got *or* (have) gotten	getting
give	gave	(have) given	giving
go	went	(have) gone	going
grow	grew	(have) grown	growing
hang	hung**	(have) hung	hanging

---

* Note that *flied* is correctly used in baseball terminology: *The batter **flied** out.*

** *Hang* meaning "to suspend by the neck" is a regular verb with principal parts *hang, hanged, (have) hanged,* and *hanging.*

Base Word	Past	Past Participle	Present Participle
hide	hid	(have) hidden	hiding
hit	hit	(have) hit	hitting
hurt	hurt	(have) hurt	hurting
keep	kept	(have) kept	keeping
know	knew	(have) known	knowing
lay	laid	(have) laid	laying
lie*	lay	(have) lain	lying
pay	paid	(have) paid	paying
ride	rode	(have) ridden	riding
ring	rang	(have) rung	ringing
rise	rose	(have) risen	rising
run	ran	(have) run	running
see	saw	(have) seen	seeing
set	set	(have) set	setting
shake	shook	(have) shaken	shaking
shine	shone	(have) shone *or* (have) shined	shining
sing	sang	(have) sung	singing
sit	sat	(have) sat	sitting
slide	slid	(have) slid *or* (have) slidden	sliding
speak	spoke	(have) spoken	speaking
steal	stole	(have) stolen	stealing
stink	stank *or* stunk	(have) stunk	stinking
swim	swam	(have) swum	swimming
swing	swung	(have) swung	swinging
take	took	(have) taken	taking
teach	taught	(have) taught	teaching
tear	tore	(have) torn	tearing
throw	threw	(have) thrown	throwing
wear	wore	(have) worn	wearing
write	wrote	(have) written	writing

* These parts apply only to the meaning "to recline or rest." Parts of *lie* meaning "to speak falsely" are *lie*, *lied*, *(have) lied*, and *lying*.

PRINCIPAL PARTS OF IRREGULAR VERBS
(GROUPED BY PATTERN)

Base Word	Past	Past Participle
Form remains unchanged.		
bet	bet	(have) bet
burst	burst	(have) burst
cost	cost	(have) cost
cut	cut	(have) cut
hit	hit	(have) hit
hurt	hurt	(have) hurt
set	set	(have) set
shed	shed	(have) shed
shut	shut	(have) shut
split	split	(have) split
spread	spread	(have) spread
	-ew	**(have) -own**
blow	blew	(have) blown
draw	drew	(have) drawn [*a* instead of *o*]
fly	flew	(have) flown
grow	grew	(have) grown
know	knew	(have) known
throw	threw	(have) thrown
long vowel	**-o-consonant-e**	**(have) -o-consonant-en**
break	broke	(have) broken
choose	chose	(have) chosen
drive	drove	(have) driven [*i* instead of *o*]
freeze	froze	(have) frozen
ride	rode	(have) ridden [*i*; doubled *d*]
speak	spoke	(have) spoken
steal	stole	(have) stolen
write	wrote	(have) written [*i*; doubled *t*]
-ake	**-ook**	**(have) -aken**
mistake	mistook	(have) mistaken
shake	shook	(have) shaken
take	took	(have) taken

Base Word	Past	Past Participle
-ay	**-aid**	**(have) -aid**
lay	laid	(have) laid
pay	paid	(have) paid
-i	**-a**	**-u**
begin	began	(have) begun
drink	drank	(have) drunk
ring*	rang	(have) rung
sing	sang	(have) sung
swim	swam	(have) swum
-ink/ing	**-ank/g *or* -unk/g**	**(have) -unk *or* ung**
shrink	shrank *or* shrunk	(have) shrunk *or* (have) shrunken
sink	sank *or* sunk	(have) sunk
spring	sprang *or* sprung	(have) sprung
stink	stank *or* stunk	(have) stunk
	-un(g)	**(have) -un(g)**
cling	clung	(have) clung
fling	flung	(have) flung
spin	spun	(have) spun
sting	stung	(have stung
swing	swung	(have) swung
wring	wrung	(have) wrung

* Note that *bring* does not follow this pattern. The past and past participle of *bring* are *brought* and *have brought*.

CONFUSING VERB PAIRS

Some verbs with similar meanings are easily confused. Three pairs are especially troublesome: *sit* and *set*, *rise* and *raise*, and *lie* and *lay*. Clearly understanding the meaning of each verb and knowing its principal parts will help you to use these words correctly.

Sit—Set

Base Word	Past	Past Participle	Present Participle
sit	sat	(have) sat	sitting
set	set	(have) set	setting

Sit means "to rest, often on the haunches." *Set* means "to put or place." *Set* is used with a direct object; *sit* is not.

*Zach **sits** near the front of the room.*

*We **sat** quietly, waiting for the play to begin.*

*The cat **has sat** on the windowsill each morning.*

(puts)   DO
*Kayla **sets** her books on the table when she gets home.*

(put)   DO
*Tony **set** the clean towels on the table.*

(put)   DO
*Mom has **set** the thermostat at 74 degrees.*

Rise—Raise

Base Word	Past	Past Participle	Present Participle
rise	rose	(have) risen	rising
raise	raised	(have) raised	raising

Both of these verbs have to do with "going up." *Rise* means "to get up" or "to go up." Something *rises* by itself. *Raise* means "to lift up" or "to put up." Like *set*, *raise* takes a direct object. (Notice that *raise* is a regular verb.)

Heat **rises**.

The audience **rose** when the star walked onto the stage.

The ash has **risen** from the volcano.

(lift)   **DO**
Raise your hand if you agree.

(put up)   **DO**
*The scouts **raised** the flag at dawn.*

(brought up) DO
*The committee **has raised** questions about the applicant's qualifications.*

45

Lie—Lay

Base Word	Past	Past Participle	Present Participle
lie	lay	(have) lain	lying
lay	laid	(have) laid	laying

This is probably the most confusing of all verb pairs, because the past form of *lie* is identical to the base word *lay*. Understanding the meaning of each base word and knowing the principal parts of each verb will enable you to use these words correctly.

Lie means "to recline" or "to rest." It's something one does to oneself. *Lay*, like *set* and *raise*, means "to put or place." *Lay* is used with a direct object. Notice that once you *lay* something down, it *lies* there.

"**Lie** down, Fritz," Kelly commanded.

Yesterday I **lay** on the beach for an hour. [past of *lie*]

Nicole **has lain** awake for two hours.

(resting)
The coats are **lying** on the bed.
[present participle of *lie*]

(put)　　**DO**
Please **lay** your coat on the bed. [present of *lay*]

(put)　　**DO**
I forget where I **laid** the map.

(put)　　　**DO**
Mandy **has laid** out the clothes she will wear tomorrow.

(putting down)　　**DO**
Our neighbors **are laying** new carpet in their house today.

May—Can

Both *may* and *can* are helping verbs. *May* means "to be allowed." It is also used to express a possibility.

> ***May*** *I go to the bathroom?*

> *You **may** want to consult this book often.*

Can means "to have the ability, power, right, or qualifications."

> ***Can*** *you lift 300 pounds?*

> *The President **can** veto bills passed by Congress.*

Teach—Learn

Teach means "to instruct; to give knowledge or skill." *Learn* means "to receive instruction; to *get* knowledge or skill."

> *Mrs. Nolte **taught** us how to figure compound interest.*

> *We **learned** how to figure compound interest.*

Borrow—Lend or Loan

Borrow means "to use something temporarily with the owner's permission." *Lend* and *loan* mean "to give someone permission to use something temporarily."

> *May I **borrow** your pencil?*

> *Will you please **lend** me your pencil?*

> *Will you please **loan** me your pencil?*

Bring—Take

Bring means "to carry toward the speaker." *Take* means "to carry away from the speaker." The correct verb, then, depends on <u>the position of the speaker in relation to the action</u>.

*"Be sure to **bring** your science project home,"* Dad reminded. [If Dad is at home, the project will be moving toward him.]

*"Be sure to **take** your science project home,"* the teacher reminded. [If the teacher is at school, the project will be moving away from her.]

USING PRONOUNS

Just as a verb must agree with its subject, a pronoun must agree with the noun it stands for. Additional problems involving pronoun usage may occur in deciding whether to use a subjective or objective pronoun. Becoming familiar with the chart of pronouns on page 5 and understanding when each type of pronoun is appropriate will help you to use pronouns correctly.

AGREEMENT WITH ANTECEDENT

In order for your speech or writing to be clear, a pronoun must agree with the noun it replaces. The noun and pronoun must agree in <u>person</u> (first, second, or third), <u>number</u> (singular or plural), and <u>gender</u> (masculine, feminine, common, or neuter). A pronoun of **common** gender (such as *they*, *them*, *our*, and *your*) can refer to both masculine and feminine. A pronoun of **neuter** gender (such as *it, its, they,* and *them*) refers to *things,* which are neither masculine nor feminine.

The noun usually precedes the pronoun. It's called the pronoun's **antecedent** (from the Latin words *ante,* meaning "before," and *cede,* meaning "go").

> *Asha rode **her** bicycle to school.* [*Her* refers to *Asha*— third person, singular, feminine.]

> *Mike and Lindsey left **their** project at home.* [*Their* refers to *Mike and Lindsey*—third person, plural, common.]

> *Many trees shed **their** leaves in autumn.* [*Their* refers to *trees*—third person, plural, neuter.]

Agreement between a pronoun and its antecedent is most likely to become a problem when indefinite pronouns are used. Study the lists on page 33 to learn which indefinite pronouns are singular and which are plural. Remember that words such as *everyone* and *everybody* are singular and, therefore, require singular pronouns.

> *Everyone forgot **his** lunch.* [*His* refers to *everyone*— third person singular.]

Until recently, *his* was widely accepted to refer to all people, both masculine and feminine, in such situations. Today many people believe that a feminine pronoun should be used half the time. This can result in awkward alternating between masculine and feminine throughout a piece of writing, or in the cumbersome repetition of "his and her," "she and he," etc. Since English has no third person singular pronoun of common gender, there is no clear solution to this dilemma. Sometimes people try to solve the problem by substituting *their* for *his:* *Everyone forgot their lunch.* Although the problem of gender is solved, these pronouns do not agree in number, since *everyone* is singular and *their* is plural. Often the best solution is to make the sentence plural:

> *All of the people forgot their lunches.*

SUBJECTIVE PRONOUNS

Subjective pronouns (often called nominative pronouns) are used as the subject of a sentence and after a linking verb.

> *They cleaned up the litter along the highway.*
>
> *It was I who discovered the clue.*
>
> *Who saw you at the mall?*

Problems with subjective pronouns are most likely to occur with a compound subject. To decide if a pronoun is correct, test it as the only subject of the sentence.

> *She and I enjoyed the play.* [Out of courtesy, first person is listed last.]
>
> *She enjoyed the play.* [NOT *Her enjoyed the play.*]
>
> *I enjoyed the play.* [NOT *Me enjoyed the play.*]

Note that in third person present tense you'll need a different verb form as you change from plural to singular to test your pronoun.

> *He and Adam play soccer.*
>
> *He plays soccer.* [NOT *Him plays soccer.*]

If a noun referring to the same person or thing immediately follows the pronoun, drop the noun to test for correct pronoun usage.

> *We girls practice field hockey every day after school.*
>
> *We practice field hockey every day after school.*
> [NOT *Us practice field hockey every day after school.*]

Although a phrase such as *we girls* is acceptable for emphasis or clarification, a pronoun should not be used immediately *after* a noun subject. Use either the noun or the pronoun.

NONSTANDARD:	*My brother he* taught me to juggle.
STANDARD:	*My brother* taught me to juggle.
STANDARD:	*He* taught me to juggle.

OBJECTIVE PRONOUNS

Some people have the mistaken impression that subjective pronouns are better than objective pronouns. These people often *make* errors as they attempt to *avoid* them. In fact, neither kind of pronoun is better than the other; each has its own important job to do.

Objective pronouns are used as direct objects, indirect objects, and objects of prepositions.

*We found **him** hiding behind a tree.* [direct object]

*She brought **us** coins from India.* [indirect object]

*Mrs. Lopez showed the bones to **them**.* [object of preposition]

*To **whom** is the letter addressed?* [object of preposition]

***Whom** <u>did</u> <u>you</u> <u>see</u> at the mall?* [direct object; question affects normal word order]

Problems are most likely to occur when you have a compound object. Considering each part of the compound object individually can help you to choose the correct pronoun.

*Ms. Schaffer asked **him** and **me** to water the plants.*
[Out of courtesy, first person is listed last.]

*Ms. Schaffer asked **him** to water the plants.*
[NOT *Ms. Schaffer asked **he** to water the plants.*]

*Ms. Schaffer asked **me** to water the plants.*
[NOT *Ms. Schaffer asked **I** to water the plants.*]

51

*Mr. Lee read **us** and **them** a story.*

*Mr. Lee read **us** a story.* [NOT *Mr. Lee read **we** a story.*]

*Mr. Lee read **them** a story.* [NOT *Mr. Lee read **they** a story.*]

Dropping the noun immediately following a pronoun that refers to the same thing is an effective test for correct pronoun usage.

*It was a secret just between **us girls**.*

*It was a secret just between **us**.*

You should never use a subjective pronoun and an objective pronoun together in a compound. Since elements of the compound must have the same grammatical structure, they will either both be subjects or both be objects.

NONSTANDARD: ***Him and I** went to the party.* [The pronouns are the subjects of the sentence. *I* is a subject pronoun, but *him* is not.]

STANDARD: ***He and I** went to the party.* [Both pronouns are correctly used as subjects.]

NONSTANDARD: *The letter was for **her and I**.* [The pronouns are used as objects of the preposition *for*. *Her* can be an object, but *I* cannot.]

STANDARD: *The letter was for **her and me**.* [Both pronouns are correctly used as objects.]

PRONOUNS IN INCOMPLETE COMPARISONS

Sometimes pronouns are used in comparisons that aren't completely stated. In order to choose the correct pronoun, you must be able to supply the implied words and notice whether the pronoun is used as a subject or an object.

*Shelly is taller than **I** [am tall].* [*I* is the subject of the implied clause.]

*Tim likes Ben more than **I** [like Ben].* [The subject *I* suggests the implied clause.]

*Tim likes Ben more than [he likes] **me**.* [Since we are given an object, we look for an implied subject and verb. Compare this example with the previous one to notice how the choice of pronoun completely changes the meaning of the sentence.]

USING MODIFIERS

Modifiers are words that describe. To use modifiers correctly, you must be sure that you use the right part of speech as well as the right form of the modifier. Placing the modifier as close as possible to the word it describes usually helps to make your writing clearer.

ADJECTIVE OR ADVERB?

Sometimes an adjective is incorrectly used as an adverb. The confusion is most likely to occur between adjectives that modify nouns or pronouns and tell "what kind," and adverbs that modify verbs and tell "how."

Many adverbs are formed by adding the *-ly* suffix to adjectives.

Adjectives (Describe Nouns)	Adverbs (Describe Verbs)
careful (driver)	(drive) careful**ly**
harsh (words)	(speak) harsh**ly**
easy (job)	(complete) easi**ly**
lazy (person)	(lounge) lazi**ly**

A few short words, such as *soft*, *loud*, *quick*, and *slow*, can be used as either adjectives or adverbs. These words also have other adverb forms that have the -ly suffix: *softly, loudly, quickly, slowly*. The adverb form having the suffix is usually used in formal situations.

Good—Well

Probably the adjective–adverb pair that causes greatest confusion is *good* and *well*. *Good* is an adjective; *well* is usually an adverb.

> *She did a **good** job on her math test.* [*Good* describes the noun *job*, telling "what kind" of job.]

> *She did **well** on her math test.* [*Well* tells "how" she did, describing the verb.]

Good should be used after a linking verb. (See page 8.)

> *The soup smells **good**.* [*Good* describes the noun *soup*.]

> *The news is **good**.* [*Good* describes the noun *news*.]

Well meaning "in good health" is an adjective.

> *I don't feel **well**.* [While *well* may seem to be an adverb describing *feel*, it's actually an adjective describing *I*. *Feel* is a linking verb. The subject isn't performing an action.]

COMPARISON OF ADJECTIVES

Many adjectives have three forms: positive, comparative, and super-lative. Understanding these forms will help you to use modifiers correctly.

The **positive** form is used if only one thing is being described.

> *Kevin is a **kind** boy.*

The **comparative** form is used to compare two people or things.

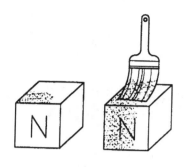

*Luis is **kinder** than Kevin.*

*Of the two boys, who is **kinder**?*

*Luis is **kinder** than anyone else in the class.* [At first this might appear to be a comparison involving more than two people. However, *anyone* is singular; Luis is being compared with only one person at a time.]

Use of *than* indicates a comparison between *two* people or things.

The **superlative** form is used if more than two people or things are being compared.

*Toby is the **kindest** boy in the school.*

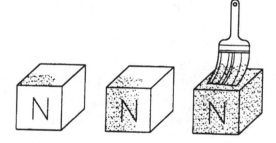

*Of all the boys, Toby is the **kindest**.*

The preceding examples show the most common way of comparing adjectives: *-er* is added to the positive to form the comparative, and *-est* is added to the positive to form the superlative. Adding these suffixes sometimes requires simple spelling changes. (See pages 93 through 95 for more information about spelling rules.)

Some words, especially those with more than two syllables, would become awkward to pronounce if these suffixes were added. Instead, longer words (and even a few two-syllable words) are compared by using the word *more* instead of the *-er* suffix and the word *most* instead of the *-est* suffix.

The following chart compares a variety of adjectives. Since there are thousands of adjectives, this list merely provides examples.

Positive	Comparative	Superlative
clean	cleaner	cleanest
bold	bolder	boldest
white	whiter	whitest
sad	sadder	saddest
pretty	prettier	prettiest
wealthy	wealthier	wealthiest
useful	more useful	most useful
famous	more famous	most famous
beautiful	more beautiful	most beautiful
valuable	more valuable	most valuable

The -er or -est suffix is never used with *more* or *most*; one or the other is used. In other words, a comparison such as *more taller* would be nonstandard. In addition, if a suffix is used to form the comparative, a suffix is also used to form the superlative. If *more* is used to form the comparative, *most* is used to form the superlative.

A few adjectives change their form completely when they are compared. Such irregular forms can be found in the dictionary entry for the positive form of the word.

Positive	Comparative	Superlative
good	better	best
bad	worse	worst
many	more	most
much	more	most
few	fewer	fewest
little*	less *or* lesser	least
far	farther *or* further	farthest *or* furthest

*This comparison is used for *little* meaning "small amount." *Little* meaning "small in size" is compared regularly.

These irregularly compared adjectives can cause special problems. *Many* and *few* are used to describe plural things. *Much* and *little* are used to describe singular things of which a part is considered.

*I have **many assignments** to complete tonight.* [*Many* describes the plural noun *assignments*.]

*I have **much homework** to complete tonight.* [*Much* describes the singular noun *homework*.]

***Few thunderstorms** occur in the desert.* [*Few* describes the plural noun *thunderstorms*.]

***Little rain** falls in the desert.* [*Little* describes the singular noun *rain*.]

The words *less* and *least* are used to show a negative comparison.

*Kevin is **less kind** than Luis.*

Particularly troublesome are the comparative adjectives *fewer* and *less*. *Fewer* should be used to describe plural things; *less* should be used to describe singular things.

***Fewer people** than we expected attended the program.* [*Fewer* describes the plural noun *people*.]

*Because we had a snack after school, there were **fewer grapes** for dinner than we wanted.* [*Fewer* describes the plural noun *grapes*.]

*Because we had a snack after school, there was **less fruit** for dinner than we wanted.* [*Less* describes the singular noun *fruit*.]

*Because of the drought, there is **less water** in the river than usual.* [*Less* describes the singular noun *water*.]

Notice that some adjectives have no comparative form because the qualities they describe do not exist in degrees.

perfect   dead   square   round   unique

Something is either perfect or it isn't; it can't be *more perfect* or *less perfect*. The phrases *nearly perfect* and *more nearly perfect* may be used, however, to describe something approaching perfection.

COMPARISON OF ADVERBS

Like adjectives, adverbs have three forms: positive, comparative, and superlative. The positive form is used to describe one action.

> *Melissa works **fast**.*

The comparative form is used to compare two actions.

> *Stephanie works **faster** than Melissa [works].*

The superlative form is used to compare more than two actions.

> *Of all students in her group, Haley works **fastest**.*

The comparative form of some adverbs is made by adding *-er*, and the superlative form of those same adverbs is made by adding *-est*. However, many adverbs already have an *-ly* suffix; adding an additional suffix would make them awkward to pronounce. Therefore, the comparative and superlative forms of most adverbs use the words *more* (or *less*) and *most* (or *least*).

The following chart compares a variety of adverbs.

Positive	Comparative	Superlative
slow	slower	slowest
slowly	more slowly	most slowly
early	earlier	earliest
noisily	more noisily	most noisily
gracefully	more gracefully	most gracefully
well	better	best

MAKING COMPARISONS LOGICAL

When making a comparison, be sure you're comparing the things you mean to compare.

ILLOGICAL: *Is **television advertising** more effective than **radio**?* [The two elements being compared here are *television advertising* and *radio*. Although *radio* can be compared with *television*, it cannot logically be compared with *television advertising*.]

LOGICAL: *Is **television advertising** more effective than **radio advertising**?* [*Television advertising* is compared with *radio advertising*.]

LOGICAL: *Is **advertising on television** more effective than **advertising on radio**?* [*Advertising on television* is compared with *advertising on radio*.]

Avoid the following additional kind of illogical comparison.

ILLOGICAL: *Matt is neater than anyone in the class.* [If Matt is a member of the class, he can't possibly be neater than himself.]

LOGICAL: *Matt is neater than anyone **else** in the class.*

ILLOGICAL: *Aleta likes the giraffe better than any animal.* [Obviously, the giraffe itself is an animal.]

LOGICAL: *Aleta likes the giraffe better than any **other** animal.*

DOUBLE NEGATIVES

In math you may have learned that two negatives often make a positive. This is also true in language.

Nobody doesn't like Sara Lee.

The two negatives (*nobody* and *n't* in *doesn't*) make a positive. The writers of this familiar slogan discovered a clever, memorable way to express the idea that everyone *does* like their product. What they really mean is *Everybody **does** like Sara Lee.*

Sometimes people use two negatives in everyday speaking or writing, perhaps intending to emphasize their negative idea. In fact, use of the double negative reveals a lack of standard usage in addition to misleading the audience.

The following words are negative. You should use only one of them (not two) to express a negative idea.

no	never	nothing
not (n't)	no one	hardly
none	nobody	scarcely

NONSTANDARD: *I don't have **no** money.* [two negatives]

STANDARD: *I don't have any money.* [one negative]

STANDARD: *I have **no** money.* [one negative]

NONSTANDARD: *She **never** does **nothing** to help me.*
[two negatives]

STANDARD: *She **never** does anything to help me.*
[one negative]

STANDARD: *She does **nothing** to help me.*
[one negative]

NONSTANDARD:	*I could**n't hardly** hear him.* [two negatives]
STANDARD:	*I could **hardly** hear him.* [one negative]
STANDARD:	*I could**n't** hear him.* [one negative]

SPECIAL SITUATIONS WITH MODIFIERS

A few modifiers may require special attention in order to be used correctly.

A—An

Use *a* before a word beginning with a consonant sound and *an* before a word beginning with a vowel sound. This makes the words easier to pronounce.

> *Steve had **an o**range and **a b**anana for lunch.*

> *We played hockey for **an** hour.* [Although *hour* starts with a consonant, the *h* is silent. *An* is used because *hour* starts with a vowel *sound*.]

Some words, such as those beginning with a "long *u*" sound, can be tricky. *Uniform* and *unicorn* are two examples. The "long *u*" sound that you hear at the beginning of these words starts with the same sound that you hear in *yellow*. This is the *consonant* sound of *y*. *Uniform* and *unicorn*, therefore, should be preceded by *a* rather than *an*.

This—That—These—Those

In using these adjectives, remember that *this* and *that* are singular; *these* and *those* are plural. In addition, *this* and *these* refer to objects nearby; *that* and *those* refer to things farther away. The meanings of the adjectives themselves already give information about the location of the noun described. Therefore, it is unnecessary (and nonstandard) to use *this here* and *that there*.

61

*The notebook on **this** desk is mine.* [one desk nearby]

*The notebook on **that** desk is yours.* [one desk far away]

[near — plural]   [far — plural]
***These** flowers look fresher than **those** flowers.*

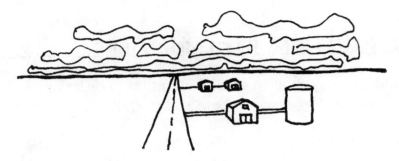

***This** farm has a grain bin; **that** farm does not.*

Errors often occur when the noun modified is *kind* or *sort*. When one of these nouns is singular, it must be preceded by a singular adjective, regardless of other plural words that may be included in the sentence.

*I have never seen **this kind** of vase before.* [singular]

***Those kinds** of animals belong in the zoo.* [plural]

Remember that the word *them* is an objective pronoun, not an adjective. It should be used to *replace* a noun, not to *describe* a noun.

NONSTANDARD: ***Them** colored pencils are mine.*

STANDARD: ***Those** colored pencils are mine; I bought **them** yesterday.*

POSITION OF MODIFIERS

In order to make your communication clear, place modifying words and phrases as close as possible to the words they modify. Notice, for example, how the meaning of a sentence changes completely as *only* is moved to different positions.

> He **only seemed** interested in science. [He wasn't really interested.]

> He seemed interested **only in science**. [He didn't seem interested in anything else.]

> **Only he** seemed interested in science. [No one else did.]

Misplaced phrases may result in humorous, misleading sentences.

> MISLEADING: *The fire was put out before any damage was done **by the local fire department**.* [Since *by the local fire department* modifies *was put out*, it should be placed closer to that phrase.]

> CLEAR: *The fire was put out **by the local fire department** before any damage was done.*

> MISLEADING: *I saw an **owl walking home from school**.* [Since the phrase follows *owl*, it sounds as if the owl is walking.]

> CLEAR: ***Walking home from school**, I saw an owl.* [The participial phrase is now next to the word it describes.]

A participial phrase (either present or past) that begins a sentence should modify the subject of that sentence.

> MISLEADING: ***Giggling uncontrollably**, the elevator took us to the sixth floor.* [The participial phrase *giggling uncontrollably* should modify the subject, which is *elevator*. Since elevators can't giggle, the sentence should be revised.]

CLEAR: ***Giggling uncontrollably**, we took the elevator to the sixth floor*. [The subject was changed to be the word modified by the participial phrase.]

CLEAR: *While **we were giggling** uncontrollably, the elevator took us to the sixth floor*. [The participial phrase was expanded to a full clause with a subject of its own.]

MISLEADING: ***Disappointed and exhausted**, the **bus** carried us home from the game*. [The past participles, *disappointed* and *exhausted*, should modify the subject, *bus*. Since this is illogical, the sentence should be revised.]

CLEAR: ***Disappointed and exhausted**, we rode the bus home from the game*. [The subject was changed to be the word modified by the participial phrase.]

CLEAR: ***We were** disappointed and exhausted as we rode the bus home from the game*. [The participial phrase was expanded to a clause with a subject of its own.]

64

MECHANICS

Mechanics involves the nitty-gritty details of written language: capitalization, punctuation, and spelling. If attention is not paid to these details, meaning can be difficult—or even impossible—to figure out.

Although each word in the following paragraph is spelled correctly, the paragraph has no punctuation or capitalization. See if you can find two completely different ways to punctuate the paragraph. They'll result in two completely different meanings. (Remember that sentences don't need to start with the subject.)

Memorable Students

they are the memorable students in any class they participate fully in any mischief they see no point in volunteering for extra jobs they delight in distracting their classmates they take no pleasure in learning they are never satisfied

---

Knowing the rules of mechanics will help you to understand what you read. Applying those rules in your own writing will help you communicate your ideas to others.

CAPITALIZATION

In general, words that are capitalized are proper nouns—words that name <u>particular</u> people, places, things, or ideas.

1. Capitalize the names and initials of people and pets. Titles, such as *Mr.*, *Ms.*, and *Dr.*, are also capitalized. Titles of relatives are capitalized when they're used as *names*. If they're simply used as words and are preceded by modifiers such as *a*, *this*, or *my*, they're lower-cased.

   Shannon studied music with Dr. Scott E. Bauer.

   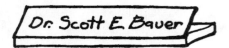

   *We left our bird, **Bangles**, with **Aunt Carol** while we visited **our grandma**.*

2. Always capitalize the word *I*. (Be sure you don't get into the habit of capitalizing other short words, such as *is* and *it*, that also begin with *i*.)

   *On our trip **I** navigated for Mom, who drove the car.*

3. Capitalize the first letter of each sentence.

4. Capitalize names of days of the week, months of the year, and holidays. Do *not* capitalize the names of seasons.

   *The latest that **Labor Day** can occur in the United States is **Monday**, **September** 7.*

   *I like the pastel flowers of **spring** and the crimson leaves of **autumn**.*

September						
S	M	T	W	Th	F	S
		1	2	3	4	5
6	Labor Day 7	8	9	10	11	12
13	14	15	16	17	18	19
20	21	22	23	24	25	26
27	28	29	30			

5. Capitalize names of towns, cities, states, countries, planets, galaxies, etc. The word *earth* is capitalized only when it refers to our planet and isn't preceded by a modifier, such as *the* or *our*.

The words *sun* and *moon* aren't capitalized, because they're common nouns rather than proper nouns.

*My family used to live in **Miami**, **Florida**.*

*Astronauts went from the **earth** to the **moon** and back.*

***Venus** and **Earth** are known as twin planets.*

6. Capitalize the names of streets, mountains, and bodies of water. Notice that most of these names contain more than one word. <u>Be sure to capitalize all words in the name.</u>

*Union Station is located on **Market Street**.*

*We flew over the **Rocky Mountains** and the **Great Salt Lake**.*

7. Capitalize names of businesses, organizations, governmental bodies, and buildings.

*The new product manufactured by **Monsanto** has been approved by the **Food and Drug Administration**.*

*Our **Girl Scout** troop went to the top of the **Gateway Arch**.*

*The **Senate** and the **House of Representatives** make up **Congress**.*

8. Capitalize words that refer to God, religions, denominations, and religious books. The word *god* is capitalized only when it refers to the Supreme Being.

*The sacred scripture of **Islam** is the **Koran**.*

***Methodists**, **Presbyterians**, **Roman Catholics**, and **Baptists** all believe in the **Bible**.*

*The ancient Greeks believed in many **gods**, **Zeus** being the most powerful.*

9. Capitalize proper adjectives made from proper nouns.

   ***American**, **European**, **African**, **Asian**, and **Australian** athletes compete in the Olympics.*

   *He ordered **French** toast, and I ordered **Spanish** rice.*

After many years of use, a term may seem so far removed from the proper adjective that a lowercase letter replaces the capital. Lowercase letters are now preferred in the terms *arabic numerals* and *roman numerals*. For a term such as *French fries,* which is in transition, it's important that you decide whether or not you will capitalize it—and then be consistent throughout a piece of writing.

10. Capitalize words that refer to particular groups of people, such as tribes or races. (When the word *black* or *white* is used to refer to race, it usually isn't capitalized.) The word *Indian* is always capitalized, whether it refers to a Native American or to someone from the country of India.

    *The **Navajo** and **Apache** tribes made their home in the southwestern United States.*

    *The first **Negroes** came to the United States in 1619.*

    *Rosa Parks pioneered in obtaining rights for **blacks**.*

11. Capitalize names of historical events, periods, documents, and prizes.

    *The period of rebuilding the South after the **Civil War** was called **Reconstruction.***

    *The **Declaration of Independence** is displayed in Washington, D.C.*

    *Will an American win a **Nobel Prize** this year?*

12. Capitalize names of vehicles—ships, planes, spacecraft, cars, trains, etc. (Names of particular vehicles—but not types of vehicles—should also be italicized or underlined.)

> *Charles Lindbergh flew from New York to Paris in the* **Spirit of St. Louis**.

> *According to legend, Casey Jones died trying to bring the* **Cannonball** *in on time.*

> *The* **Toyota Corolla** *is a popular import.*

13. Capitalize trade names but not the common nouns indicating the type of product.

> *I bleached my* **Levi jacket** *in* **Clorox**.

14. Capitalize titles when they're used with a name or in place of a name. Don't capitalize these words when they're used as common nouns. (An exception is the noun *president*, which is usually capitalized when it refers to the President of the United States.) Also capitalize the abbreviation of a degree following a person's name.

> **Mayor** *Rolla Wells helped to bring the World's Fair to St. Louis in 1904.*

> *What is your opinion of the new ordinance,* **Mayor**?

> *We visited* **the mayor's office** *on our field trip.*

> *Who will be the next* **President** *of the United States?*

> *The black bag belongs to Lisa Collins,* **M.D.**

15. In general, capitalize abbreviations of words that would be capitalized. Don't capitalize abbreviations of words that wouldn't be capitalized. (Few abbreviations are acceptable in formal writing.)

> *The* **U.S.** *Department of Agriculture provides assistance to farmers.*

*A person's normal body temperature is 98.6 degrees **F**.*

*6 **ft**. 4 **in**.*

16. Capitalize direction words only when they designate geographic regions. Don't capitalize them when they merely indicate direction.

    *The **Middle East** has been an area of unrest for thousands of years.*

    *The **South** is more industrialized than it used to be.*

    *We traveled **west** for 2,000 miles to get to California.*

17. Don't capitalize school subjects unless they name languages or particular numbered courses (as in college).

    *We study **math**, **science**, **social studies**, **English**, **music**, **art**, and **Spanish**.*

    *According to my placement test, I should register for **Math 186**.*

18. Capitalize the first letter of a direct quotation. Don't capitalize the first letter of a continuing quotation when the tag (the words identifying the speaker) occurs in the middle of a sentence. (For information about punctuating direct quotations, see pages 85–87.)

    *Jessica asked, "**Where** are my blue socks?"*

    *"**Where**," Jessica asked, "**are** my blue socks?"*

19. In titles of books, poems, songs, stories, etc., capitalize the first letter of the first word, the last word, and all other important words. Verbs and pronouns are usually considered to be important. Words that aren't considered important are articles (*a*, *an*, and *the*), coordinating conjunctions (*and*, *but*, *or*, etc.), and prepositions of fewer than five letters. (For more information about setting off titles, see pages 87 and 88.)

*The guest of honor was reunited with people he or she hadn't seen in years on **This Is Your Life**.*

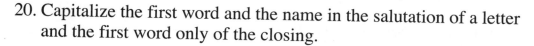

*Everyone stood to sing **"The Star-Spangled Banner"** before the ball game began.*

Around the World in Eighty Days *is a fascinating book by Jules Verne.*

20. Capitalize the first word and the name in the salutation of a letter and the first word only of the closing.

> ***Dear Grandpa**,*
>
> > ***Your** nephew,*
>
> ***Dear Ms. Tanaka**:*
>
> > ***Yours** truly,*

21. In outlines, capitalize the first word of each main head and sub-head. (For information on outline form see pages 129–131.)

22. Capitalize the first word of each line of poetry. (Many modern poems do not follow this traditional form.)

> ***Quietly** I watched the rain*
> ***Trickle** down the window pane.*

PUNCTUATION

One meaning of *punctuate* is "to interrupt at intervals." Stars "punctuate" the night sky; cheers may "punctuate" a speech. Likewise, punctuation marks break up a block of writing, making it easier to understand.

Periods, question marks, exclamation points, commas, semicolons, and colons directly follow a word (without an intervening space). Therefore, they <u>should never be used at the beginning of a line of writing</u>.

PERIOD •

1. Use a period at the end of a declarative or imperative sentence.

    Today is a very warm day. [declarative]

    Please open the window. [imperative]

    Some sentences involving speculation are really declarative or imperative, requiring a period rather than a question mark.

    I wonder what time it is. [declarative]

    Guess how much this costs. [imperative]

    People sometimes use question form for requests to which they don't expect a spoken reply. This kind of request should be followed by a period rather than a question mark.

    Will the audience please stand.

2. Use a period after an abbreviation or an initial. Never use more than one period at the end of a sentence.

    *Our next-door neighbor is **R. W. Garcia, M.D.***

    The United States Postal Service prefers that everyone use two-letter state abbreviations in addresses. Both letters of these abbreviations are capitalized, and no periods are used. In sentences, however, the names of states are generally spelled out.

    MN = Minnesota   **ME** = Maine

QUESTION MARK **?**

Use a question mark at the end of an interrogative sentence.

    What time is it?

Some sentences have the grammatical form of a statement, but the way they are spoken (or intended to be read) indicates that they are questions. A question mark should be used after such a sentence.

You found your science book in the refrigerator?

On the other hand, some requests have the grammatical form of a question even though no spoken reply is expected. This kind of request should be followed by a period.

Will you please return the form by Monday.

Some sentences involving uncertainty are really declarative or imperative rather than interrogative. They require a period rather than a question mark.

I wonder how many stars are in the sky. [declarative]

Guess how many beans are in the jar. [imperative]

EXCLAMATION POINT !

1. Use an exclamation point at the end of a sentence that shows surprise or strong feeling. (Note that the form of the sentence may be declarative or imperative.)

   What an exciting game it was! [exclamatory]

   It's snowing! [declarative]

   Watch out for that hole in the ground! [imperative]

2. Use an exclamation point after an interjection that shows strong feeling.

   Ouch! You stepped on my toe.

A comma is used to set off certain information within a sentence. Words that are closely related, such as subject and verb, adjective and noun, and preposition and object, generally won't be separated by a comma. Separating various elements helps to make the independent clause stand out so that the main idea of the sentence is easier for the reader to find and understand.

If you know the reasons for using commas, you'll more easily understand what you read, and other people will more easily understand what you write. Simply putting a comma "where you would pause" is not a reliable guide. Understanding punctuation rules will help you punctuate more quickly and confidently.

1. Use a comma to separate the name of a city or town from the name of a state or country. If this appears in the middle of a sentence, use a comma after the state or country also.

   *We went to **Chicago, Illinois,** to explore the museums.*

   Don't use any punctuation between the state and the ZIP code.

   ***Boise, ID** 83708*

2. Use a comma to separate the day from the year. If this appears in the middle of a sentence, use a comma after the year also.

   *On **July 20, 1969,** the first person landed on the moon.*

   If only the month and year are used, no commas are needed.

   *The **July 2001** issue of <u>LinguaPhile</u> included an article about vision.*

3. Use a comma after the salutation (or greeting) of a friendly letter.

   Dear Heather,

4. Use a comma after the closing of any letter.

   Your friend,

5. Use a comma after a last name that precedes a first name, as on a form or in a list.

   Henderson, Susan E.

6. In a series of <u>three or more items</u>, use a comma after each item except the last. Don't use a comma before the first item.

   *She bought **a hammer, a screwdriver, and a wrench**.*

   Many sources will say that the comma before *and* is unnecessary. While this comma is often optional, it's sometimes needed to clarify meaning—and it's never wrong. If you use it regularly, you won't have to decide whether it's needed in specific situations.

   Sometimes a series is part of a phrase that begins with *such as*. This phrase should be set off with commas *if* it provides *extra* information (if the basic meaning of the sentence would be the same even without that phrase).

   *Basic tools**, such as a hammer, a screwdriver, and a wrench,** are essential in any home.* [Because the examples are <u>not necessary</u>, the phrase is set off by commas. The main idea of the sentence is *Basic tools are essential in any home.*]

   A phrase introduced by *such as* might provide *necessary* information, however. In that case, the phrase shouldn't be set off by commas.

   *Animals **such as the woolly mammoth, the giant short-faced bear, and the North American cheetah** have become extinct.* [Because the examples are <u>necessary</u> to indicate which animals are meant, no commas are used. Omitting this phrase would greatly change the meaning of the sentence: *Animals have become extinct.* Notice that simply adding the word *Some* at the beginning of the sentence would cause the phrase to be extra information and would require the use of commas.]

7. If two or more adjectives describe the same noun and they could appropriately be connected with *and*, use a comma between them. These are sometimes called **coordinate adjectives**.

> The **capable, hard-working** *student usually excels.*
> [Both *capable* and *hard-working* describe *student*.]

If the first adjective modifies the idea of the second adjective and the noun together, the adjectives aren't coordinate, and a comma shouldn't be used. If one of the adjectives describes shape, material, or color, the comma probably isn't appropriate.

> The **large delivery truck** *blocked the street.* [No comma is used because you wouldn't say *large and delivery truck. Large* describes *delivery truck*, not just *truck*.]

8. Use a comma before the conjunction in a compound sentence. (For more about compound sentences, see page 19.)

> *He wanted to see the show,* **but** *he had band practice at the same time.*

Note that a comma is not used if only the verb is compound.

> *He* **wanted** *to see the show but* **had** *band practice at the same time.*

A comma shouldn't be used if the clauses are joined with *so that*, which is a subordinating, rather than a coordinating, conjunction. Sometimes the *that* is only implied rather than stated. If you're unsure about using the comma, try substituting *so that* for *so*. If the meaning of your sentence remains unchanged, omit the comma.

> *I set my alarm* **so** *I'd be sure to wake up on time.*
> [IMPLIED: *I set my alarm* **so that** *I'd be sure to wake up on time.* The second clause is dependent, so no comma is used.]

9. Use a comma to separate a direct quotation from its tag (the words that identify the speaker). Note the position of the commas in relation to the quotation marks.

Alicia asked, "What is the problem?"

"What," *Alicia asked,* "is the problem?"

If the tag follows a quotation that's a question or an exclamation, a question mark or exclamation point is used instead of a comma.

"What seems to be the problem?" Alicia asked.

10. Use a comma after an introductory word, such as *yes*, *no*, or *well*.

   Yes, I'd love to go to the state fair tomorrow.

11. Use commas to set off an expression that begins, ends, or interrupts a sentence. Examples of such expressions are *too, of course, however, for example, by the way, on the other hand, in my opinion, don't you,* and *nevertheless.* (Note that *too* is set off by commas only when it means "also," not when it indicates an excess.)

   He would like to visit Hawaii, too.

   He, too, would like to visit Hawaii.

   I am too tired to begin that job now.

   You realize, of course, that I'm kidding.

   I enjoy water skiing, don't you?

   By the way, I saw the new movie you recommended.

Use a period or semicolon instead of a comma if the expression comes *between* independent clauses rather than within a clause.

   <u>We</u> <u>tried</u> to lift the rock; *however*, <u>it</u> <u>would</u> not <u>budge</u>. [This is a compound sentence. If the semicolon were replaced with a comma, it would be a run-on.]

   We pulled up the small tree. The rock, however, would not budge. [However comes in the middle of a clause and simply needs to be set off by commas.]

77

12. Use commas to set off the <u>name of a person spoken to</u>. This is called **direct address**.

> *Jason, would you please help me?*
>
> *If you wait, Amber, I'll go with you.*
>
> *What do you want, Mother?*

13. Use commas to set off an **appositive** that includes *extra* information. An appositive is a noun or noun phrase that names the same thing as a noun or noun phrase right next to it in the sentence.

> *The person who lives next door to me is **Chris, my best friend**.* [*Chris* and *my best friend* name the same person.]
>
> ***Chris, my best friend,*** *lives next door to me.*

Notice that each sentence would be complete and would have the same basic meaning if the appositive were omitted; the reader just wouldn't have as much information.

Sometimes an appositive includes information that is *necessary* rather than extra. In that case, commas shouldn't be used.

> *My son Nathan refinished my grandfather's rolltop desk.* [Since commas aren't used, we know that *Nathan* is necessary information—that there's more than one son.]
>
> *My son, Nathan, refinished my grandfather's rolltop desk.* [The use of commas indicates that *Nathan* is extra information; therefore, he must be the only son.]

In situations such as the one above, the reader must rely on correct punctuation to get the correct meaning from the sentence.

14. Prepositional phrases are generally not set off by commas. However, you might use a comma after a long introductory prepositional phrase or series of phrases.

> **In the deepest recess of the cave,** *the bear slept for the winter.*

You should definitely use a comma if it is necessary in order to prevent misreading.

LIKELY TO BE MISREAD: *In the summer days seem to pass quickly.* [On first reading it's unclear whether *summer* is a noun or an adjective.]

REVISED FOR CLARITY: *In the summer,* *days seem to pass quickly.* [The comma clarifies that *summer* is the object of the preposition *in.*]

15. Use a comma after a dependent clause at the beginning of a sentence. (For a list of subordinating conjunctions, which often begin dependent clauses, see page 13.)

> **As the car sped away,** *the witness quickly jotted down the license number.*

A dependent clause at the end of a sentence is usually not set off by a comma. A comma may be used, however, if information in the dependent clause contrasts strongly with information presented earlier in the sentence.

> *The witness quickly jotted down the license number* **as the car sped away.**

> *I will go along with your plan,* **although I will be surprised if it works.**

16. Use a comma to set off adjectives or other elements that, due to unusual word order, seem to be outside the main clause.

*In the pit we found the puppy, **cold and whimpering**.*

***Cold and whimpering**, the puppy cowered in the pit.*

*The puppy, **cold and whimpering**, cowered in the pit.*

17. Use a comma to separate a **participial phrase** or **absolute phrase** from the rest of a sentence. These **non-restrictive** phrases contain extra information that is <u>not necessary</u> to the basic meaning of the sentence.

> ***Frightened by the gunshot**, the horse reared, **throwing its rider to the ground**.* [past and present participial phrases]

> ***His eyes glued to his book,** he pretended not to hear her.* [absolute phrase. An absolute phrase, which modifies an entire clause, includes a subject and a partial predicate.]

Each sentence would be complete without the non-restrictive phrase; it just wouldn't be as descriptive. A comma in this type of sentence helps to call attention to the independent clause, the part of the sentence that contains the most important information.

18. Use a comma to set off a **non-restrictive clause**. A non-restrictive clause is one that provides <u>extra information</u>.

> *Saturn, **which is the sixth planet from the sun,** is known for its rings.*

In the sentence above, removing the clause set off by commas wouldn't change the basic meaning of the sentence; the reader would simply be missing one piece of information.

A **restrictive** clause—one that is <u>necessary</u> to the meaning of the sentence—should not be set off by commas.

> *Meat **that has been unrefrigerated for several days** is unfit to eat.* [The boldface clause is restrictive. It's necessary to explain (or restrict) which meat is meant. Eliminating the restrictive clause completely changes the meaning of the sentence: *Meat is unfit to eat.*]

Which usually introduces a non-restrictive clause, which provides <u>extra information</u> and has <u>commas</u>. *That* usually introduces a restrictive clause, which has <u>necessary</u> information and <u>no commas</u>.

The current trend in punctuation is toward an open, rather than a closed, style. This means that optional commas are likely to be omitted. Some people omit commas in short compound sentences or after short dependent clauses. Be sure that punctuation is making your writing easier to understand, not unnecessarily complicating it.

SEMICOLON ;

A semicolon provides punctuation that is stronger than a comma but not as strong as a period. It's used to separate elements that are <u>grammatically equal</u>.

1. Use a semicolon to separate clauses of a compound sentence that aren't connected with a coordinating conjunction.

   <u>*Pepper*</u> <u>*makes*</u> *me sneeze;* <u>*onions*</u> <u>*make*</u> *me cry.*

   A semicolon is equal to a comma plus a coordinating conjunction.

   $$; \; = \; , \; + \; \textbf{and}$$

   You should *not* use a semicolon to join unequal elements, such as a dependent clause and an independent clause.

   Like anything special, semicolons become less effective when they are overused. They can be helpful, however, to show that some ideas in a paragraph are more closely related than others. The explanations in this book (not just the examples) illustrate the appropriate use of the semicolon and other punctuation marks.

2. If commas are used within items in a series or within clauses in a compound sentence, use a semicolon instead of a comma to separate the items or clauses. This stronger punctuation helps to show the stronger breaks within the sentence.

On our vacation we visited Springfield, Missouri;
Springfield, Illinois; and Springfield, Ohio.

I enjoy woodworking, stamp collecting, and swimming;
but my sister likes singing, dancing, and acting.

COLON

1. Use a colon to separate the hours from minutes in writing time.

    2:35 p.m.

2. Use a colon after the salutation in a business letter.

    Dear Ms. Schwartz:

3. Use a colon to introduce a list <u>that follows an independent clause</u>.

    These are the supplies I need: paper, pencils, and pens.

    Don't use a colon between the verb and its direct object.

    INCORRECT: *For school I need: paper, pencils, and pens.*

    CORRECT: *For school I need paper, pencils, and pens.*

APOSTROPHE

The apostrophe works differently from other punctuation marks. The apostrophe is *within* a word rather than *between* words. Correct use of the apostrophe is more a matter of spelling than of punctuation.

1. Use an apostrophe to replace omitted letters in a contraction.

    doesn't [does n**o**t]   you've [you **ha**ve]

    hasn't [has n**o**t]   o'clock [**of the** clock]

2. An apostrophe is used to make the **possessive** form of a noun. The possessive form is used to show ownership. Follow these steps to determine where to place the apostrophe.

    a. Ask yourself (in these words) TO WHOM DOES [ITEM] BELONG?

    b. Notice whether the answer to your question ends in an *s* you can hear (not a silent *s*).

    c. If the word doesn't end in *s*, or if the *s* is silent, add **'s**; if the word ends in an *s* you can hear, add only an apostrophe.

Example 1: hats belonging to a lady

a. TO WHOM DO THE HATS BELONG? *lady*

b. *Lady* doesn't end in *s*.

c. *'s* is added: *lady's hats*

Example 2: hats belonging to the ladies

a. TO WHOM DO THE HATS BELONG? *ladies*

b. *Ladies* does end in an *s* you can hear.

c. Only an apostrophe is added: *ladies' hats*

Example 3: toys belonging to children

a. TO WHOM DO THE TOYS BELONG? *children*

b. *Children* doesn't end in *s*.

c. *'s* is added: *children's toys*

Example 4: the army of Xerxes [zûrk´ zēz]

a. TO WHOM DOES THE ARMY BELONG? *Xerxes*

b. *Xerxes* does end in an *s* you can hear.

c. Only an apostrophe is added: *Xerxes' army*

Example 5: the capital of Arkansas

a. TO WHAT DOES THE CAPITAL BELONG? *Arkansas*

b. *Arkansas* ends in *s*, but the *s* is silent.

c. *'s* is added: *Arkansas's capital*

For nouns and names ending in *s*, an *s* may be added after the apostrophe if you prefer a second *s* sound in the word:

    boss**'s** policy   Ross**'s** flag

    duchess**'s** wig   Jones**'s** house

<u>Note that these are possessives, not plurals.</u> You'd be unlikely to add this extra *s* if the possessive noun has another *s* in it and if the thing owned begins with an *s*.

Moses' staff for Je**sus' s**ake

When two or more people own something together, only the last-named noun should have the possessive form.

Will Chloe and Jenna's house be on the tour?
[The house belongs to both Chloe and Jenna.]

If ownership is not joint, however, each noun should be possessive:

Chloe's and Jenna's houses were on the tour.
[Chloe and Jenna have separate houses.]

With the exception of the compounds above, the apostrophe affects only an <u>individual noun</u>. Trying to make a whole phrase possessive usually results in a sentence that is awkward if not humorous:

INCORRECT: *I got the recipe from the girl who gave the picnic's grandmother.* [The sentence should be worded so that the grandmother clearly belongs to the girl rather than to the picnic.]

You can often avoid awkward possessives by rewording your sentence and using the word *of* instead of an apostrophe.

REVISED: *I got the recipe from the grandmother of the girl who gave the picnic.*

3. Use an apostrophe to write the plural of a letter or a symbol.

<u>Mississippi</u> has four i's and four s's.

His address has five 1's in it.

<u>Remember that the apostrophe is not used in forming other plurals.</u>

84

HYPHEN   —

As with the apostrophe, correct use of the hyphen is mainly a matter of spelling.

1. Use a hyphen in some compound words and in two-word numbers from twenty-one to ninety-nine. A dictionary will show you which compound words to hyphenate.

    jack-of-all-trades   mother-in-law

2. Use a hyphen when two or more words combine to make an adjective.

    *The girl who won **first place** is **ten years old**.*

    *A **ten-year-old girl** won the **first-place award**.*

    This rule applies to fractions. A fraction used as an adjective should be hyphenated; a fraction used as a noun should not be.

    *a **two-thirds** majority*   [adj.]

    ***two thirds** of the voters*   [n.]

3. If a word won't fit on a line, use a hyphen to divide the word <u>at the end of a syllable</u>. You see an example of this in Item #2 above. Note that the hyphen goes after the first part of the word at the end of the line; the following line doesn't start with a hyphen. One-syllable words shouldn't be divided. (To learn more about dividing words into syllables, see pages 121–124.)

QUOTATION MARKS   " "

Quotation marks are used in pairs. Since there's no space between an opening quotation mark and the word that follows it, an opening quotation mark shouldn't end a line of writing. Similarly, a closing quotation mark shouldn't begin a line of writing.

1. Use quotation marks to enclose <u>exact words spoken</u>.

> ***"Where are you going?" Mom asked.***

> *Mom asked,* ***"Where are you going?"***

The tag, indicating the speaker, is separated from the quotation by a comma unless a question mark or an exclamation point is used. <u>A comma shouldn't be used right next to a question mark or exclamation point.</u>

Notice that the first word of a direct quotation begins with a capital letter. If a tag is placed in the middle of a quoted sentence, however, the first letter following the tag is lowercase.

> *"Where," Mom asked, "are you going?"*

If a tag is placed between sentences within a quotation, end punctuation is used either before or after the tag. The new sentence starts with a capital letter.

> *"Where are you going?" Mom asked. "You need to clean your room."*

> *"Where are you going?" Mom reminded, "You need to clean your room."*

If a direct quotation is longer than one sentence, place opening quotation marks at the beginning, and closing quotation marks at the end. Don't enclose each sentence individually.

> ***"Where are you going? You need to clean your room,"*** *Mom reminded.*

When writing a conversation involving two or more people, <u>start a new paragraph whenever you change speakers</u>. Study the dialogue on the next page to see how these rules are applied.

Mom asked, "Where are you going, Mark?"
"Over to Raul's house to play," Mark replied.
"You must be forgetting that you need to clean your
room before our company arrives," Mom reminded.
"Aw, gee," Mark grumbled, starting upstairs.

Don't use quotation marks if you're reporting what someone said without using exact words. This is called an **indirect quotation**. The word *that* often signals an indirect quotation.

> *Mom reminded me **that** I needed to clean my room.*

If a quotation continues over several paragraphs (such as a story within a story), begin each new paragraph with opening quotation marks even though you have not used closing quotation marks. This reminds the reader that the material is quoted.

2. Use quotation marks to enclose titles of poems, stories, songs, and articles. In general, quotation marks are used for the titles of short pieces that would likely be part of a longer work. <u>Notice that these titles are not set off with commas.</u>

> *Our Great Books group discussed **"The Nightingale."***

3. Use single quotation marks for a quotation or a title within a quotation.

> *"Have you memorized **'Paul Revere's Ride'**?" Erica asked.*

> *"Sam said, **'I refuse to go!'**" Kim reported to Dani.*

<u>Commas and periods are always placed inside closing quotation marks.</u> Question marks and exclamation points are placed inside if they're part of the quotation or title; otherwise they're placed outside. <u>Colons and semicolons</u> are always placed <u>outside</u> closing quotation marks. These rules are illustrated in explanations and examples throughout this book.

UNDERLINING (ITALICS)

1. Underline (or italicize) the title of a book, newspaper, magazine, play, or movie. In general, underlining is used for titles of longer works or for collections of shorter works. Titles of sacred writings and government documents require neither quotation marks nor underlining. (Since example sentences are already italicized, elements that should be italicized are underlined below.)

    > **_The Lord of the Rings: The Return of the King_** *is an action-packed film with remarkable special effects.*

    > *Did you read "The President's Toughest Decision" in a recent issue of* **_Parade_***?*

    > *Many people memorize passages from the* **Constitution** *and from the* **Bible***.*

2. Underline the name of a <u>specific</u> ship, train, spaceship, etc.

    > *The* **_Titanic_** *was supposed to be unsinkable.*

    > *The explosion of the* **_Columbia_** *was a tragedy.*

3. Underline a word or phrase requiring special emphasis. The less often you use this, the more effective it will be. If you try to emphasize too much, you'll end up emphasizing nothing; everything will look the same. Too much underlining also tends to make writing look juvenile. Instead, you can emphasize by word choice or by other means of punctuation.

    > INEFFECTIVE: *I was* **_not_** *offended by what* **_you_** *said.*

    > EFFECTIVE: *I was not offended by what you said.*
    > [This emphasis suggests that someone else might have been offended.]

4. Underline a word or phrase from another language.

    > *Carpe diem* (kär ´ pə dē ´ əm) *means "Seize the day"; make the most of the time you have.*

88

5. Underline a word, letter, or other symbol if you're referring to the word or symbol itself rather than to the *meaning* it generally has. This is something you may not use often; however, you see many examples of it in this book.

> *In formal writing you should spell out __and__ rather than use __&__ (called an ampersand).* [In this sentence *and* means "the word *and*"; it does not carry *and*'s usual meaning or perform its usual function.]

PARENTHESES ( )

Parentheses are used to enclose information that could be omitted without changing the basic meaning of the sentence. We've seen that commas can serve this purpose as well. If you're trying to decide whether to use parentheses or a pair of commas, keep in mind that commas are less interruptive than parentheses. If the extra information is closely related to the sentence and commas make the meaning clear, you should use commas. If the extra information is more removed from the sentence or if meaning is unclear with commas (perhaps because you have other commas in the sentence), you should use parentheses. Parentheses enable you to add information that might be difficult to fit into the grammatical structure of a sentence.

Like quotation marks, parentheses are always used in pairs (one side of a pair of parentheses is called a **parenthesis**). One advantage of parentheses over commas or dashes (to be discussed later) is that they alert your reader to the *end* of a detour as well as to the beginning.

When using parentheses within a sentence, begin the enclosed material with a lowercase letter. This is illustrated in the paragraph above.

If the enclosed material is a question or exclamation, punctuate it accordingly (within the parentheses).

> *We spent two hours (__every minute worthwhile!__) waiting in line to ride the Excalibur.*

Don't use a period inside the parentheses, however, unless the parenthetical material is not enclosed in any other sentence.

> *The team wasn't in top form. (This was their first game*
> *of the season.)*

If the parenthetical expression is inserted where a punctuation mark is
needed in the sentence, the punctuation mark comes after—not
before—the parenthetical expression.

> *Because it rained **(three inches!)**, the race was postponed.*

When using parentheses, be sure the sentence would be complete and
logical if the parenthetical expression were omitted.

> ILLOGICAL: *You are an even better **(more versatile***
>   ***player)** than I realized.*

> LOGICAL: *You are an even better **(more versatile)***
>   *player than I realized.*

The frequent use of parentheses shows an immature writing style and is
likely to distract the reader. Always consider whether your sentence
would be better if the parenthetical information were either omitted or
included in the main part of the sentence.

> *We were tired after our long drive **(twelve hours)**.*

> *We were tired after our twelve-hour drive.*

DASH   —

1. A dash may be used to indicate an interruption.

> *"There seems to be something wrong with the ph—"*
> *Aaron said as the line went dead.*

2. Like parentheses, a dash may indicate a sudden shift in thought.
   Often dashes are used in pairs. Generally they're considered to be
   even <u>more interruptive than commas or parentheses</u>. Therefore,

they provide greater emphasis. Whether you use commas, parentheses, or dashes is often a matter of personal preference.

*For whatever reason—**was it courage or foolishness?**—300 Spartans battled 250,000 Persians at Thermopylae.*

If you use more than one dash within a sentence, be sure the dashes are a pair, enclosing one idea and then taking your reader back to your main train of thought. Otherwise, a series of dashes would lead your reader farther and farther off track.

Like parentheses, dashes should not be overused.

ELLIPSIS POINTS   •   •   •

Ellipsis points (sometimes simply called an **ellipsis**) consist of three periods with space between them. If you were typing ellipsis points, you'd alternate between the space bar and the period. Many keyboards now have one stroke that produces ellipsis points. This treats the points as one unit so that they don't spill over from one line to the next.

1. Like a dash, ellipsis points may be used to show interrupted speech. Often ellipsis points indicate faltering speech while a dash indicates an interruption or a shift in thought.

   "I . . . uh . . . think you're standing on my foot," the woman said.

2. Ellipsis points may indicate an omission of one or more words from quoted material. You might omit some words so that the quotation will better focus on the point you're making.

   ORIGINAL: *TV, though sometimes informative, can reduce a person's ability to think.*

   AS QUOTED: *"TV . . . can reduce a person's ability to think."*

You don't need to use ellipsis points when you quote a whole sentence (the reader would assume that the quoted matter is taken

91

from a larger context). Ellipsis points may be followed by other punctuation. If the ellipsis is at the end of a sentence, a fourth period would represent end punctuation. <u>That's the only situation in which you'd use more than three periods.</u>

Beware of ellipses (/ĭ lĭp´ sēz/, the plural of *ellipsis*) used in advertising. The omission of certain words might have significantly changed the meaning of the quotation.

BRACKETS — [ ]

Brackets, which occur in pairs, may be used when you need to clarify the meaning of a quotation by adding or substituting words that weren't in the original. Your version should in no way change the meaning or intent of the original material.

> *"The third President of the United States made a shrewd purchase [the Louisiana Territory] that doubled the size of the country."*

You might also put some words in brackets so that your quotation will blend more smoothly with the surrounding text.

> *"[Thomas Jefferson] made a shrewd purchase that doubled the size of [the United States]."*

Although the previous examples show how to use brackets, the sentence would be better if it were reworded so that the quotation marks, and therefore the brackets, were unnecessary.

> *Thomas Jefferson purchased the Louisiana Territory, which doubled the size of the United States.*

SPELLING

You'll probably find it helpful to break longer words into smaller parts to spell them. You might spell words one syllable at a time (see pages 121–124), or you might think about the units of meaning that make them up (see pages 109–117). Knowing a few rules about adding prefixes and suffixes will help you spell thousands of words.

1 + 1 + 1 RULE

If a one-syllable word ends with one consonant preceded by one vowel, double the consonant before adding a suffix <u>beginning with a vowel</u>.

s t **o p** + **p** + [vowel suffix] = sto**pp**ed, sto**pp**ing

s t **a r** + **r** + [vowel suffix] = sta**rr**ed, sta**rr**ing

If the suffix begins with a consonant, simply add the suffix without doubling the consonant.

g l **a d** + [consonant suffix] = gla**dl**y

Notice that the final consonant is *not* doubled if a root word ends in two consonants or in one consonant preceded by two vowels.

h e **l p** + [vowel suffix] = he**lp**ed, he**lp**ing

c l e **a** n + [vowel suffix] = clea**n**ed, cleaning

The *u* following a *q* does not count as a vowel. Words with a *qu* followed by only one vowel and one consonant follow the 1 + 1 + 1 rule.

q u **i z** + **z** + [vowel suffix] = qui**zz**ed, qui**zz**ical

1 + 1 + 1 APPLICATION FOR TWO-SYLLABLE WORDS

When adding a vowel suffix to a two-syllable word ending in a single consonant preceded by a single vowel, double the consonant <u>if the second syllable is accented</u>.

b e g **i n** + **n** + [vowel suffix] = begin´ning

o c c **u r** + **r** + [vowel suffix] = occur´red, occur´ring, occur´rence

r e f **e r** + (**r**) + [vowel suffix] = refer´red, refer´ring, ref´erence

Notice in the last example above that the *r* is not doubled when the accent is on the first syllable.

WORDS ENDING IN SILENT *E*

When a word ends with a silent *e*, drop the *e* before adding a suffix <u>beginning with a vowel</u>.

h o p **e** + [vowel suffix] = hop**ed**, hop**ing**

Notice that the silent *e* is usually kept before a suffix <u>beginning with a consonant</u>.

hop**eful**   car**eless**   lon**ely**   mov**ement**   fals**ehood**

There are a few common EXCEPTIONS to this rule:

tru**ly**   argu**ment**   whol**ly**   judg**ment**   acknowledg**ment**

A silent *e* is kept before a suffix beginning with *a* or *o* if that *e* is needed to keep a "soft" *c* or *g* from having a "hard" sound. (The letters *c* and *g* are generally "hard" before *a*, *o*, *u*, and consonants.)

mana**ge** + able = mana**ge**able

noti**ce** + able = noti**ce**able

94

WORDS ENDING IN *Y*

Words ending in *y* preceded by a consonant generally change *y* to *i* before all suffixes *except* those beginning with an *i*.

tr**y̶** + [suffix] = tr**ies**, tr**ied**
    i

eas**y̶** + [suffix] = eas**ier**, eas**iest**, eas**ily**
    i

happ**y̶** + [suffix] = happ**ier**, happ**iest**, happ**iness**
    i

beaut**y̶** + [suffix] = beaut**iful**, beaut**ify**
    i

The *y* is kept before a suffix beginning with *i*.

trying carr**ying** stud**ying** bab**yish** lobb**yist**

In words where *y* is preceded by a vowel, the *y* is kept, whether the suffix begins with a vowel or with a consonant.

k**ey**s pl**ay**ed ob**ey**ing j**oy**ful empl**oy**ment

A common EXCEPTION to the preceding rule is *paid* (root word: *pay*).

PLURALS

The plural of a noun is the form of the word that indicates more than one. Unless a noun forms its plural by following one of the first two rules discussed below, you could find the plural form in the dictionary entry for that noun. The plural, identified with *pl.*, usually appears in boldface type near the beginning of the entry.

1. Most nouns form their plural simply by adding *s*.

day day**s**   elephant elephant**s**

smile smile**s**   chimney chimney**s**

2. Nouns that end in *s*, *sh*, *ch*, *x*, or *z* form their plural by adding *es*. This adds an extra syllable that makes the words pronounceable.

dress	dress**es**		chur**ch**	chur**ches**
bru**sh**	bru**shes**		box	box**es**
			walt**z**	walt**zes**

3. Nouns that end in *y* preceded by a consonant form their plural by changing *y* to *i* and adding *-es*.

i cit~~y~~	cit**ies**	**i** countr~~y~~	countr**ies**
i la**d**~~y~~	la**dies**	**i** famil~~y~~	famil**ies**

4. Most nouns that end in *f* or *fe* form their plural by adding *s*. Some such nouns form their plural by changing *f* or *fe* to *ves*. In most cases, you can hear a *v* in the plural when the word is pronounced correctly.

gul**f**	gul**fs**		chie**f**	chie**fs**
belie**f**	belie**fs**		loa**f**	loa**ves**
hal**f**	hal**ves**		thie**f**	thie**ves**
wol**f**	wol**ves**		li**fe**	li**ves**
kni**fe**	kni**ves**		sel**f**	sel**ves**
wi**fe**	wi**ves**		lea**f**	lea**ves**

5. Nouns that end in *o* preceded by a vowel usually form their plural by adding *s*.

rad**io**	rad**ios**		pat**io**	pat**ios**
z**oo**	z**oos**		rod**eo**	rod**eos**

Nouns ending in *o* preceded by a consonant generally form their plural by adding *-es*.

he**ro**	hero**es**	toma**to**	tomato**es**
ve**to**	veto**es**	mosqui**to**	mosquito**es**

Many EXCEPTIONS to the preceding rule are words that have to do with music. They form their plural simply by adding *s*.

al**to**	altos	pia**no**	pianos
so**lo**	solos	sopra**no**	sopranos

Some nouns ending in *o* preceded by a consonant have two correct spellings for their plural forms. When a dictionary shows alternatives, the preferred form is usually given first.

ze**ro**	zeros *or* zeroes	torna**do**	tornados *or* tornadoes
ho**bo**	hobos *or* hoboes	volca**no**	volcanos *or* volcanoes

6. Some nouns form their plural irregularly.

man	men	louse	lice
woman	women	foot	feet
child	children	tooth	teeth
mouse	mice	goose	geese

7. Some nouns don't change their spelling from singular to plural.

deer   sheep   trout   moose   salmon

A few nouns have two correct spellings for their plural forms, one that is identical to the singular form and another that is formed in the regular way.

fish *or* fishes	shrimp *or* shrimps
pair *or* pairs	youth *or* youths

8. Some nouns that have come to English from other languages form their plurals irregularly. Some have two correct forms.

alumnus	alumni	larva	larvae
analysis	analyses	phenomenon	phenomena
crisis	crises	phylum	phyla
datum	data	radius	radii *or* radiuses
formula	formulas *or* formulae	stadium	stadiums *or* stadia
		stimulus	stimuli

9. Most compound nouns written as one word form their plural in the usual way. However, hyphenated and open compounds usually form their plural by adding the suffix to the part of the word that actually increases in number.

cupful	cupfuls	son-in-law	sons-in-law

10. The rules governing the pluralization of names are simpler than those governing the pluralization of many nouns: Depending on the ending of the name itself, form the plural by adding *s* or *es*.

Robert	Roberts	Roberts	Robertses
Mary	Marys	Charles	Charleses
Marie	Maries	Jones	Joneses

Always identify the singular form of the noun so that you'll form the plural correctly. Notice that these plurals have no apostrophes.

If a correct construction seems awkward to you, you can often avoid the plural by rewording.

The Roberts Family [instead of *The Robertses*]

Two girls in our club are named Mary.

ADDING PREFIXES

Generally a prefix is added without changing the spelling of the root word. The chart on pages 110–117 will help you know the spellings of both prefixes and roots. Notice that if a root begins with the same letter a prefix ends with, the new word will have a double letter.

un	+	necessary	=	un**n**ecessary
over	+	rule	=	ove**rr**ule
il	+	legal	=	i**ll**egal
dis	+	appear	=	di**s**appear
dis	+	satisfy	=	di**ss**atisfy

WORDS EASILY CONFUSED

When words have similar spellings, people need to find ways to remember which spelling to use in each situation. Sentences or illustrations, such as those used here, might help you to remember correct spellings. Try creating some of your own!

1. **accept—except**

   Accept means "to receive."

   Please __accept__ this __pac__kage.

   Except means "leaving out; but."

   All __exits__ __except__ one were blocked.

2. **advice—advise**

   Advice (ăd vīs´) is a noun.

   She was __nice__ and gave me good __advice__.

Advise (ăd vīz´) is a verb.

*I will ask the wise person to **advise** me.*

3. **affect — effect**

Affect is a verb meaning "to act on; to change."

*How do holidays **affect** the mood of the staff?*

Effect is usually a noun meaning "result."

*What is the **effect** of sunlight on plant growth?*

Effect is occasionally used as a verb meaning "to make happen; to bring about."

*Because the cancer was discovered early, doctors were able to **effect** a cure.*

4. **angel — angle**

Angel means "a heavenly being." [Notice that *g* followed by *e* has a "soft" sound.]

*Angela portrayed an **angel** in the pageant.*

Angle means "the shape made when two straight lines meet." [Notice that *g* followed by a consonant has a "hard" sound.]

*The triangle had three 60-degree **angles**.*

5. **are — our**

Many people pronounce these words the same. However, more precise pronunciation may help you to use the words correctly.

Are (är) is a form of the verb *to be.*

*You **are** my best friend.*

Our (our—*ou* as in *out*) is a possessive pronoun.

O<u>ur</u> h<u>ou</u>se is on the corner.

6. desert—dessert

Desert (dĕz´ ûrt), as a noun, means "an area getting little rain."

*Camels used to be known as the "ships of the **desert**."*

Desert (də zûrt´), as a verb, means "to leave; to abandon."

*The frightened soldier was tempted to **desert** the army.*

Dessert (də zûrt´) means "the final course of a meal." You might remember that *dessert* has an extra *s* because dessert is something extra at a meal.

*We had peach cobbler for **dessert**.*

7. every day—everyday

Every day is two words meaning "each day."

***Every day** I get up at 7:00.*

Everyday is an adjective meaning "ordinary; not special."

*Meeting a famous person is not an **everyday** event.*

8. have—of—off

Have is a verb, often a helping verb.

*You should **have** recycled those aluminum cans.*

The substitution of *of* for *have* is most likely to occur after *could*, *should*, or *would*. In speech we often contract the words. We say *could've*, for example, which sounds like "could of." "Could of" is never correct, however. Even "could've" is likely to be seen only in writing dialogue.

Of (ŭv) is a preposition.

*My little brother got a new box **of** crayons.*

Off (ôf) is a preposition or an adverb. It should not be used with *of.*

*I brushed the fly **off** my arm.*

*The plane took **off** at noon.*

9. **it's—its**

It's is a contraction for *it is.*

***It's** a beautiful day.*

Its is a possessive pronoun. A look at the pronoun chart on page 5 will remind you that *no* possessive pronoun uses an apostrophe. Perhaps that will help you to remember not to use one in *its.*

*The chair is uneven because **its** leg is broken.*

10. **know—now**

Know (nō)

*Do you **know** the answer?*

Now rhymes with *cow.*

*The <u>cow</u> is **<u>now</u>** in the pasture.*

11. **loose—lose**

Loose (lo͞os) means "not tight."

*Her t<u>oo</u>th is **l<u>oo</u>se**.*

Lose (lo͞oz) means "to mislay" or "to suffer loss."

*Be careful not to **lose** the r<u>ose</u>.*

*We don't want to **lose** the game.*

12. passed—past

Passed is the past tense form of the regular verb *pass.*

> *She **passed** the salt.*

> *The dieter quickly **passed** the bakery.*

As a noun, *past* refers to time that has gone by.

> *Historians study the **past**.*

Past can also be a preposition.

> *He walked <u>fast</u> **past** the <u>last</u> bakery.*

13. quit—quite—quiet

Paying careful attention to the pronunciation indicated by the spelling pattern in these words will help you to use them correctly.

Quit (kwĭt), which follows the typical short vowel pattern, means "to stop."

> ***Quit** bothering me!*

Quite (kwīt), which follows the typical vowel-consonant-*e* pattern, means "to a great extent."

> *I felt **quite** satisfied with my essay.*

Quiet (kwī´ĕt) means "not loud." Notice that the two vowels are in different syllables.

> *It is important to be **quiet** in a library.*

14. than—then

Than is used in comparisons.

> *D<u>an</u> has a better pl<u>an</u> **than** St<u>an</u>.*

Then is used to indicate time.

K<u>en</u> *put the h*<u>en</u> *in the p*<u>en</u>*;* **then** *he w*<u>ent</u> *to the d*<u>en</u>*.*

15. **there—their—they're**

There indicates place. [Associate *there* with other "place" words that end in *ere*: *here* and *where*.]

She was already **there** *when I arrived.*

There is sometimes used to start sentences in which the subject follows the verb.

There <u>are</u> *three* <u>ways</u> *to wear this hat.*

Their is a possessive pronoun.

That house has been in **their** *family for eighty years.*

They're is a contraction for *they are*.

They're *planning to go ice skating this afternoon.*

16. **to—too—two**

To is a preposition.

He gave the book **to** *me.*

To is often used with the infinitive form of the verb.

He wants **to** *become an architect.*

Too means "also" or "more than enough." [You might remember this by thinking of the word as having "more than enough" *o*'s.]

I want to go, **too***.*

The box was **too** *large for one person to carry easily.*

Two is a number.

*I have **two** sisters.*

17. wear — where — were

Pronouncing these words correctly will help you to use them correctly.

Wear (wâr) means "to carry on the body."

*It's a great day to **wear** my new <u>earmuffs</u>.*

Where (hwâr) indicates place. [Associate *where* with other "place" words that end in *ere*: *here* and *there*.]

Where *are my tennis shoes?*

Were (wûr) is a past form of the verb *to be*.

*We **were** working in the garden when she arrived.*

18. weather — whether

Weather (wĕTH´ ûr) means "outside conditions, such as temperature, precipitation, and sunshine."

*I hope the **weather** will be nice for our picnic.*

Whether (hwĕTH´ ûr) is a subordinating conjunction expressing doubt. When the word is pronounced correctly, you'll hear a blast of air before the *w* sound. If you put your hand in front of your mouth, you should be able to feel this air, which you shouldn't feel when you pronounce *weather*.

*I have to ask my parents **whether** I can go to the mall.*

19. which — witch

The difference in pronunciation between these two words is the same as that between *whether* and *weather* discussed above.

Which (hwĭch) may introduce a dependent clause.

> *I returned the library book,* **which** *was overdue.*

Which may indicate a choice.

> **Which** *do you prefer?*

Witch (wĭch) means "a person believed to have magical powers."

> *I stitched my <u>itchy</u>* **witch** *costume for Halloween.*

20. who's—whose

Who's is a contraction for *who is.*

> **Who's** *ready to dive into the pool?*

Whose is the possessive form of *who.*

> **Whose** *jacket is this?*

21. you're—your

You're is a contraction for *you are.*

> **You're** *asking for trouble.*

Your is a possessive pronoun. Look at the pronoun chart on page 5 to remind yourself that no possessive pronoun has an apostrophe.

> *What is* **your** *favorite hobby?*

WORDS OFTEN MISSPELLED

Check this list often so that you'll spell these words correctly. Add other words that are troublesome for you.

a lot	eighth	minute	soccer
again	embarrass		speech
allowed	equipment	necessary	stopped
always	every	ninety	straight
answer			studying
Arctic	February	once	supposed
argument	finally		sure
	foreign	paid	surprise
before	fortunately	perform	
beginning	forty	probably	they
bicycle	friend		through
built		ready	tired
business	government	really	tomorrow
	guess	receive	trouble
coming		recommend	
completely	happened		until
	height	safety	upon
definite		said	
describe	interesting	science	Wednesday
disappear		second	which
disappoint	judgment	sentence	woman (sing.)
doesn't		separate	women (pl.)
	knowledge	since	

COMMUNICATING IDEAS

Spend a few moments trying to think without using words.

Were you able to do that? Possibly not. The words and structure of our language determine, to some extent, how we think.

In addition to helping us think, language enables us to share ideas. Have you ever tried to communicate with someone who didn't speak or understand your language? A few ideas, such as heat, cold, or hunger, can be communicated with gestures. However, communication between people who don't share a language is quite limited.

On the other hand, *with* the tool of language, the possibilities for communication are almost endless. The author Homer of ancient Greece so precisely described the geographical features around the city of Troy that German archaeologist Heinrich Schliemann was able to locate the site nearly 3,000 years later! Many writers are able to arrange the squiggles of ink that we call letters in such a way that they move us to terror, agony, joy, or other emotions.

In this section you'll find ways to strengthen your ability to manipulate ideas, whether you are receiving those ideas through reading or are sharing your original ideas through writing. As you improve your language ability, you'll also improve your thinking skills.

VOCABULARY

As mentioned in the introduction to this book, English has acquired words from around the world. Becoming familiar with many words will help you to understand what you read. Having a large vocabulary will also make a wide selection of words available to you when you write.

If you'd add just one new word each day to your vocabulary (in addition, of course, to words assigned to you in your studies), in a year you'd have learned 365 new words! Make your family aware of *any* words you're learning—in your studies or on your own. The more you see and hear those words in sentences, the better you'll understand them. You should make an effort to *use* new words, too—in your speech and in your writing.

MORPHEMES

A **morpheme** is the <u>smallest unit of meaning</u> in a word. In many cases a whole word is a single morpheme.

> look   giraffe   school   view

Often, however, a word consists of a root or base word with prefixes and/or suffixes attached. If you know the meaning of each of these parts, you can "add them up" and figure out the meaning of the whole word. For example, the -*s* morpheme at the end of a noun indicates a plural. The -*ed* morpheme at the end of a verb indicates past tense; *re-* at the beginning of a word means "back" or "again."

> giraffe + s = giraffes   re + view + ed = reviewed

Notice that the letters themselves aren't *always* morphemes and don't always have these meanings. *Re* in *picture* or *read*, for example, isn't a morpheme. It isn't a separate unit of meaning; the two letters are simply part of a longer morpheme.

Many English morphemes originated in other languages. *Hippopotamus*, for example, combines the Greek morpheme *hippos*, meaning

109

"horse," with the Greek morpheme *potamos*, meaning "river." The hippopotamus is, literally, a "river horse."

Knowing the meanings of common morphemes can help you figure out the meanings of thousands of words the first time you see them. In the list below, a morpheme followed by a hyphen would be used at the beginning of a word as a prefix; a morpheme preceded by a hyphen would be used at the end of a word as a suffix. Since a suffix determines a word's part of speech, the part of speech is shown with each suffix's meaning. A morpheme in the list without a hyphen is a root and could have prefixes or suffixes attached to it. In some cases a morpheme has more than one spelling or the spelling might change slightly as the morpheme attaches to other parts of a word.

Morpheme and Meaning	Examples
a-, an- (not; without)	atheist, amoral, apathy, anarchy
ab- (away; from)	abnormal, abject, abrupt, abstract
-able (capable of) (adj.)	changeable, dependable, reliable
-acy (quality or state of) (n.)	privacy, delicacy, lunacy, conspiracy
ad- (to, toward)	administer, adhere, advent, admit
-al (having to do with) (adj.)	national, regional, emotional
ambi-, amphi- (both)	amphibian, ambiguity, ambivalent
anim (life; spirit)	animal, animation, unanimous
ann (year)	annual, anniversary, annuity
ante- (before)	antecedent, anteroom, antebellum
anthropo (mankind)	anthropomorphic, philanthropist
anti- (against)	antisocial, antidote, antifreeze
aqu, aqua (water)	aquarium, aquatics, aqueduct, aqua
arch (chief; principal)	archenemy, monarch, archbishop
aster, astro (star)	astronaut, asterisk, disaster, aster
-ate (cause to be) (v.)	educate, duplicate, manipulate
-ative (tending toward) (adj.)	talkative, negative, decorative

aud (hear)  auditory, audience, audit, audition

110

Morpheme and Meaning	Examples
auto- (self)	automobile, autobiography, autocrat
bene- (good; well)	benefit, benediction, benevolent
bi- (two)	bicycle, bisect, bilateral, bicameral
biblio- (book)	bibliography, Bible, bibliophile
bio- (life)	biology, biography, biodegradable
cap (head)	capital, captain, per capita, capitulate
cede, ceed (go; yield)	proceed, exceed, recede
ceive, cept (take)	deceive, accept, reception
cent (center)	central, concentric, egocentric
cent (hundred)	century, percent, centennial
chrom (color)	monochromatic, chromosome
chron (time)	chronology, chronic, anachronism
cide (kill)	homicide, suicide, insecticide
circum- (around)	circumference, circuit, circus
cise (cut)	incision, incisor, concise, precise
clam, claim (cry; shout)	exclaim, proclaim, clamor, declaim
clin (slope; lean)	incline, recline, inclination, decline
clud, clus (close; shut)	include, conclusion, preclude
co-, con-, com- (with; together)	cooperate, concur, companion
contra-, counter- (against)	contrast, counterattack, contradict
corp (body)	corpse, corporal, corporation
crat, cracy (government)	democracy, autocracy, aristocrat
cred (believe)	credibility, credit, incredible, creed
cycle (circle)	bicycle, cyclone, encyclopedia
de- (down; from)	depose, detract, describe, deduct
deca, dec (ten)	decimal, decade, decathlon, decibel
demo (people)	democracy, epidemic, demography

111

Morpheme and Meaning	Examples
derm (skin)	dermis, dermatologist, hypodermic
dia- (across; through)	diameter, dialogue, diagram, dialysis
dict (say) 	dictate, predict, verdict, diction
dis- (not; opposite)	dislike, disappear, disappoint
duc (lead)	induce, conduct, duke, educate
en-, em- (make; give)	enable, encourage, empower
-en (make; give) (v.)	sweeten, harden, strengthen
epi- (on; over)	epilogue, epitaph, epidermis
-er (more) (adj.)	louder, softer, prettier, handier
-er (one who) (n.)	baker, washer, crier, pitcher
eu- (good; well)	euphemism, euthanasia, eulogy
ex- (former)	ex-spouse, ex-president, ex-convict
ex- (out)	exhale, exit, exterior, exception
extra- (outside)	extracurricular, extraordinary
fac, fic (make; do)	factory, fiction, artifact, manufacture
fin (end; limit)	final, infinite, definition, definite
flect, flex (bend) 	reflect, deflect, inflection, flexible
flu (flow)	fluid, fluent, fluctuate, confluence
fore- (in front of; earlier)	forearm, foretell, foreshadow
form (form; shape)	inform, reform, conform, deform
fract, frag (break)	fracture, fragment, fragile
-ful (full of) (adj.)	colorful, thankful, wonderful
-fy, -ify (to make) (v.)	simplify, magnify, beautify, deify
gamy (marriage)	monogamy, bigamy, polygamy
gen (produce; beget)	generation, generous, genealogy
geo (earth)	geography, geology, geophysics

Morpheme and Meaning	Examples
gnos (knowledge)	agnostic, ignorant, diagnosis
grad, gress (step)	gradual, graduation, progress
graph, gram (write)	photograph, phonograph, telegram
-hood (state of) (n.)	childhood, statehood, likelihood
hydr-, hydro- (water)	hydrate, hydrophobia, hydrogen
hyper- (above; excessive)	hyperactive, hypercritical, hyperbole
hypo- (under; insufficient)	hypodermic, hypothesis, hypocrisy
-ible (capable of) (adj.)	divisible, legible, horrible, edible
-ic (having to do with) (adj.)	democratic, chronic, civic, enigmatic
in-, im- (in, into)	inside, include, income, import
in-, im-, il-, ir- (not)	inactive, impure, illegal, irregular
inter- (between, among)	intermission, interrupt, interject
intra-, intro- (within)	intramural, introvert, intravenous
-ion, -sion, -tion (process) (n.)	union, expression, introduction
-ish (like; somewhat) (adj.)	childish, selfish, reddish, sluggish
-ism (doctrine of) (n.)	conservatism, patriotism, criticism
-ist (one who) (n.)	artist, loyalist, dramatist, realist
-itis (inflammation of) (n.)	tonsillitis, appendicitis, sinusitis
-ity (state of) (n.)	acidity, locality, familiarity, humidity
-ive (tending toward) (adj.)	active, destructive, sensitive, native
-ize (to make) (v.)	memorize, modernize, customize

ject (throw)   inject, reject, dejected, subject

jud (law)	judge, judicial, prejudice
junc (join)	junction, conjunction, injunction
lab (work)	labor, laboratory, collaboration
-less (without) (adj.)	hopeless, careless, countless
loc (place)	locate, location, dislocate, relocate
log(ue), loc, loq (speak)	monolog(ue), elocution, colloquial

113

Morpheme and Meaning	Examples
-logy (study of)	biology, psychology, ecology
lumin, luc (light) 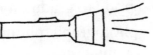	illuminate, lucid, Lucifer
-ly (in the manner of) (adv.)	slowly, freely, happily, angrily
mal- (bad)	malnutrition, malignant, malice
man (hand)	manual, manicure, manuscript
-ment (act or condition of) (n.)	government, refreshment, ornament
merg, mers (dip)	emerge, submerge, immersion
meter, metr (measure)	metric, thermometer, geometry
micro- (small)	microscope, microchip, Micronesia
mis- (wrong; ill)	mislead, misunderstand, misread
mit, miss (send)	transmit, permission, missile
mono- (one)	monotone, monologue, monorail
-mony (resulting condition) (n.)	harmony, testimony, matrimony
mort (death)	mortician, immortal, mortgage
mot, mov (move)	movie, motion, promote, mobile
multi- (many)	multiply, multitude, multicolored
-ness (condition) (n.)	kindness, happiness, rudeness
non- (not)	nonstop, nonconformist, nonfiction
nov (new)	novel, innovation, novice
ob- (in the way; against)	obstruct, object, obscure
ocu (eye)	binoculars, oculist, ocular
-oid (in the form of) (adj., n.)	asteroid, mongoloid, trapezoid
omni- (all)	omnipotent, omniscient, omnivore
-or (one who or which) (n.)	governor, conqueror, motor
-ose, -ous (full of) (adj.)	famous, porous, verbose, comatose
-osis (state of) (n.)	hypnosis, tuberculosis, osteoporosis
pan- (all; universal)	panacea, panorama, Pan-American

Morpheme and Meaning	Examples
para- (beside)	parallel, paraphrase, parasite
path (feeling)	sympathy, apathetic, pathology
ped, pod (foot)	pedal, tripod, pedestrian, impede
pel, puls (push; drive)	expel, impulse, propel, dispel
pend, pens (hang; weigh)	pendulum, suspenders, suspense
penta- (five)	pentagon, Pentateuch, pentathlon
per- (through)	perforate, perceive, perfume
peri- (around)	perimeter, peripheral, periscope
phil (love)	Philadelphia, philosophy, philatelist
phobia (fear)	claustrophobia, hydrophobia
phon (sound)	phonograph, telephone, symphony
photo (light)	photography, photosynthesis
plic (fold)	duplicate, implicate, complicate
plor (cry out)	implore, explore, deplorable
pneumo (wind, air)	pneumonia, pneumatic, pneuma
poli (city)	metropolitan, police, politics
poly- (much, many)	polygon, polyester, polygraph
pop (people)	population, popular
port (carry)	porter, import, portable, teleport
pos (to place)	pose, deposit, impose, position
post- (after)	postpone, postwar, postscript
pre- (before)	precede, precaution, prefix
press (press)	express, depress, impression
pro- (forward)	proceed, prospect, progress

115

Morpheme and Meaning	Examples
pseudo- (false)	pseudonym, pseudointellectual
psych (mind)	psychology, psychiatry, psychic
quadr-, quar (four)	quadrilateral, quadruped, quarter
quint- (five)	quintuplet, quintet, quintile
re- (back)	reverse, retrieve, return, refund
re- (again)	review, replay, recopy, rebuild
reg (guide; rule)	regulation, irregular, regime, register
retro- (backward)	retrorocket, retroactive, retrograde
rupt (break)	disrupt, interrupt, eruption, abrupt
scope (see) 	telescope, microscope, stethoscope
scrib, script (write)	prescribe, inscription, scribble
semi- (half, partly)	semicircle, semicolon, semiannual
sens, sent (feel)	sense, sensitive, sentimental, resent
-ship (quality or state) (n.)	friendship, leadership, scholarship
sist (stand)	insist, assist, exist, consist, resist
sol (alone)	solo, solitary, desolate
soma (body)	psychosomatic, somatology
spec, spic (look, appear)	inspect, spectacle, conspicuous
spir (breathe)	inspire, aspire, perspiration, expire
struct (build)	construct, destruct, instruct
sub- (under)	submarine, submit, subscribe
sult (jump)	insult, exultant, assault, result
sum (highest)	sum, summit, summary
sume, sumpt (take)	assume, consume, presumptuous
super- (over)	superlative, supersonic, superior
sym-, syn- (together)	symphony, synonym, symbol
tact, tang (touch)	contact, tangible, tactile, tangent
tain, ten, tin (hold)	contain, tenant, pertinent, detain

116

Morpheme and Meaning	Examples
tele (far)	telephone, television, telekinesis
temp (time)	temporary, contemporary, tempo
tend, tens (stretch)	extend, tension, tendency, intense
term (end)	terminate, terminal, determine
terr (land; earth)	territory, extra-terrestrial
tetra- (four)	tetrahedron, tetrad, tetrology
theo (God, god)	theology, atheism, monotheism
therm (heat)	thermometer, thermostat, thermos
tract (pull)	tractor, retractable, attract, traction

trans- (across)	transcontinental, translate, transfer
tri- (three)	tricycle, triangle, trinity, trio
-tude (quality of) (n.)	solitude, attitude, multitude, latitude
ultra- (beyond)	ultramodern, ultrasound, ultraviolet
un- (not; opposite)	unhappy, unlucky, untie, unfasten
uni- (one)	unison, unicorn, unicycle, unique
vac (empty)	vacuum, evacuate, vacation
ven (come)	adventure, intervene, circumvent
ver (truth)	verdict, verify, aver
verg (to lean)	verge, converge, divergent
vert, vers (turn)	invert, reverse, converse, version
vid, vis (see)	evidence, vision, invisible, supervisor
voc, voke (call)	vocation, vocal, invoke, revoke
volv (turn)	revolve, evolve, involve, revolution

Try combining the morphemes in different ways. Also try combining them with other morphemes. You'll increase your vocabulary!

UNDERSTANDING A DICTIONARY ENTRY

Understanding all parts of a dictionary entry can make a wealth of information available to you. Notice the parts of the entry below.

a   b c   d   e   f   g   h

arch (ärch) *n.* pl. **arch´es 1.** a curved structure which is capable of supporting the weight of material over an open space. [Doorways, windows, bridges, etc. are often **arches**.] **2.** anything curved in the shape of an arch. [the **arch** of the foot] *v.* **arched, arch ing 3.** to cause to bend into an arch. [A cat can **arch** its back.] **4.** to span, to extend an arch over. [A bridge **arches** over the river.] Arch comes from the French word *arche* which comes from the Latin word *arcus* meaning a bend or a bow.

From *Dictionary Skills* published by Milliken Publishing Co. (www.millikenpub.com)

a. The **entry word** appears in boldface type. It shows the spelling and syllable divisions of the word.

b. The **pronunciation** follows the entry word. Check the pronunciation key to learn the sounds indicated by the diacritical marks. Syllabication for pronouncing words is often different from syllabication for writing them.

c. The **part of speech** is usually indicated by an abbreviation in italics. There may be more than one part of speech.

d. **Inflections**, such as plurals of nouns or principal parts of verbs, usually appear in boldface type.

e. **Definitions** are numbered. More common definitions usually appear earlier in the entry.

f. A **sentence** may illustrate the use of the word. This may appear in brackets or italics.

g. The **origin** of the word may be shown near the beginning or end.

h. A **picture** may help clarify the meaning of the word.

WORDS IN CONTEXT

No matter how large your vocabulary is, you'll sometimes encounter words that are unfamiliar to you. Finding each of these words in a dictionary could become an arduous task—and would interrupt your reading. Learning how to use clues from the surrounding words will help you to determine the meanings of many words, even without a dictionary.

Notice the following example.

> *The peacock's* **plumage** *is very colorful.*

If you ask yourself what is "colorful" about a peacock, you'll realize that *plumage* must mean "feathers."

Sometimes, as in the following example, the sentence indicates a relationship between the unfamiliar word and a word or phrase you already know.

> *Women's* **suffrage**, *or right to vote, was granted by ratification of the Nineteenth Amendment to the U.S. Constitution in 1920.*

Sometimes you won't be able to determine a word's meaning from context. In such cases the dictionary will help you. Even when you *think* you have figured out a word's meaning, you might want to check a dictionary to confirm your guess.

DENOTATION AND CONNOTATION

Words have both denotative and connotative meanings. A word's **denotation** is the dictionary definition, the idea that the word represents. People generally agree on a word's denotation. A word's **connotation** involves the emotional associations that accompany the word. People may agree, to some extent, on a word's connotation; however, connotation will vary somewhat from one person to another.

The following words, with the same denotation, could name the same thing.

stench   odor   smell   scent   aroma   fragrance

Their connotations differ, however. *Smell* is neutral. *Stench* is the most negative, and *fragrance* is the most positive.

The words *house* and *home* have similar denotations. Both words could refer to the same building. *House* denotes "a residence for people, often for one family" and has a neutral connotation. However, *home* has a connotation that usually suggests "warmth, family, comfort." *Home* might have a negative connotation for some people.

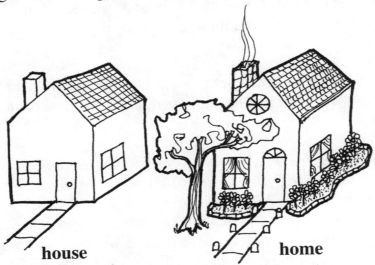

house   **home**

Being aware of words' connotations can help you communicate effectively. If you unknowingly use a word with a strong connotation, your message may be received in a way you didn't intend. Understanding connotations will help you get the full meaning from your reading.

READING

Reading is a popular leisure activity as well as an important way of getting information. Knowing word meanings, sentence structure, and mechanics will help you understand what you read. Longer passages will be easier to read if you notice how they are organized and consider how they relate to what you already know. Become an active reader!

Incidentally, one of the best ways to become a better reader is simply to read. As with playing the piano or shooting a basket, your reading skill will improve as you practice. The more you read, the better reader you'll become. The better you read, the more you'll like it. The more you like it, the more you'll do it. And so on . . . .

DECODING UNRECOGNIZED WORDS

Decoding is one of the most basic reading skills. It simply means "breaking the code," changing a word from its written to spoken form. When you first learned to read, decoding demanded most of your attention. Once you could pronounce the words, their meaning was clear to you. The words were part of your everyday vocabulary.

As you gained skill in reading, your attention probably shifted from decoding to comprehension. Although you may be able to decode most words easily, you might have trouble understanding a section of text. Maybe there are individual words or complicated sentence structures that you don't understand. Maybe the idea of the sentence is outside your experience and so makes no sense to you. Maybe you can't see the relationship between the ideas. Most of the pages in this section will help you understand what you read more easily. First, though, we'll look at steps that will help you decode words that you don't immediately recognize.

1. Know the sounds that letters represent. Although many consonants represent just one sound, each vowel (*a, e, i, o, u,* and *y*) can represent several sounds. Decoding will be easier if you know which sound a vowel is likely to represent in different situations.

   The sound a vowel makes is greatly affected by the kind of syllable it's in. A **syllable** is one beat of a word. It includes one vowel sound and perhaps consonant sounds as well. The word *friend* has only

121

one syllable. *Friendship* has two. Clapping once for each beat of a word can help you hear how many syllables a word has.

The basic rules below will help you know which sound to give the vowel in many syllables.

a. Each vowel has what is commonly called a "short vowel" sound (this has nothing to do with how long the sound lasts). The short sound of each vowel is the sound it makes in these key words:

add   **e**nd   **i**t   **o**dd   **u**p   g**y**m

A vowel is likely to make the short sound if it is the only vowel in the syllable *and* if the syllable ends with one or more consonants. A syllable that ends in this way is called a **closed syllable**. Notice that all of the key words above are closed syllables.

Here are some two-syllable words that have closed syllables:

den·tist   dis·rupt   en·rich

b. If a syllable ends with a vowel, the vowel is probably long, or says its name. (This is called an **open syllable**.)

si·lent   **pu**·pil   **lo**·**ca**·tion

c. If a syllable ends with a vowel–consonant–*e* pattern, generally the vowel is long and the *e* is silent.

con·**fuse**   com·**plete**   re·frig·er·**ate**

d. Syllables ending in *r* and syllables having two vowels together are likely to have several possibilities for their vowel sound. If you often have trouble with words like these, see page 178 or consult a book that gives more information about phonics.

2. Know how to blend sounds. For example, even if you know the sounds represented by *c*, *a*, and *t* in *cat*, you'll be unable to decode that word if you can't blend the sounds together.

3. Know how to divide a word into syllables. Although it's easier to divide words when you already know how to pronounce them, applying a few rules can help you figure out how to pronounce words that you don't immediately recognize. As you look at the example words in this section, you might also notice how they illustrate the pronunciation rules discussed on page 122.

a. Divide a compound word between the words that make it up.

flag·pole   tooth·brush   rose·bud

b. Identify prefixes and suffixes, which are usually separate syllables.

re·spect·**ful**   **pre**·scrip·**tion**   **dis**·**ap**·point·**ment**

c. Do not divide between letters of a digraph (a **digraph** is two letters that make one sound, such as *ch*, *th*, or *sh*).

an·**th**em   jac**k**·et   bu**sh**·el

d. Divide between repeated consonants.

ha**p**·**p**en   ra**b**·**b**it   let·ter

e. Use these guidelines for dividing between other consonants: Divide between consonants that don't make a blend (a **blend** is two or more consonant sounds that can be said smoothly together).

nu**t**·**m**eg   ma**g**·**n**et   vel·vet

If there are only two consonants between the vowels, sometimes even consonants that *could* be a blend are divided.

pu**b**·lic   hel·met   ba**s**·**k**et

If there are three consonants between the vowels and the middle consonant could join with either one to make a blend, the middle consonant is more likely to go with the second syllable.

chil·**dr**en   em·**bl**em   nos·**tr**il

123

f. Divide a word ending in *-le* before the consonant preceding the *l*. This rule is especially helpful in pronouncing the *first* syllable of a word. You'll see whether the syllable is open (with a long vowel) or closed (with a short vowel).

bu·**gle**　　　jug·**gle**　　　cra·**dle**

g. If you have a two-syllable word with only one consonant between two vowels, the consonant is more likely to go with the second syllable, especially if the first syllable is a prefix.

You might have to try different divisions to see which one gives you a recognizable word.

FIRST TRIAL:　　pla·net [long vowel; not recognized]
SECOND TRIAL:　　plan·et [short vowel; recognized]

Some spellings have more than one pronunciation.

pol·ish　　　Po·lish

4. The last step in decoding a word is to **accent** the right syllable. Most words have one syllable that is said more loudly than the others. Some multisyllabic words have a secondary accent as well as a main accent. Accenting the wrong syllable might keep you from recognizing a word you would otherwise know.

Some people have difficulty hearing the accent in a word; to them, all syllables sound as if they're receiving equal stress. These people are likely to also have trouble applying unequal stress in words they're trying to decode. If you have trouble with accent, exaggerate the difference in stress between the syllables. Say one syllable very loudly and others very softly. Then try to decide which version sounds most like a word you know.

A word ending in *-ion* nearly always has the accent on the syllable just before the suffix. This holds true even when the syllable is a vowel carrying little or no meaning.

ex·pres´ sion　　　in·fec´ tion　　　re·lax·a´ tion

5. Many unaccented syllables have a very slight vowel sound that's neither long nor short. This sound is called a **schwa** [shwä]; many pronunciation keys represent it by an upside-down *e* [ə]. As you can see from the boldfaced letters in the words below, any vowel letter can make a schwa sound.

a·round   la·**bel**   pen·**cil**   lem·**on**   cir·**cus**

6. Know how to interpret the pronunciation key of a dictionary so that you'll know the sounds letters are likely to have in a certain word.

Once you've decoded a word, you might find that it's a word you understand. However, if the word is unfamiliar to you, you'll still need to determine its meaning—from context clues or from a dictionary.

When you can decode easily, you'll be able to give more of your attention to comprehension—and reading will be easier for you.

S Q 3 R

The SQ3R method, explained on the following pages, will help you to read efficiently. With this method, you'll get the most from textbooks, articles, and other informative material in the shortest time.

1. **Surveying**. In surveying (or previewing) a chapter or an article, read the following:

> title
> introduction
> headings
> study aids (vocabulary, questions, graphic material, captions)
> conclusion

As you preview, begin relating what you'll read to what you already know—from previous study and from your own experience. <u>Think as you read.</u> Notice how the chapter is organized. Prepare to fit details into this general organization.

2. **Questioning**. The material itself contains some questions, and others

have probably occurred to you during your pre-viewing. Now turn each heading into a question that you might reasonably expect the section to answer. Make predictions about what will happen or what you'll learn. Of course, you might need to revise your predictions as you read.

3. **Reading**. Read each section to find answers to your questions. This gives purpose to your reading. You're not simply reading words; you're reading to find important information. The information will be easier for you to understand and remember if you constantly relate new ideas to what you already know. Making mental pictures of what you read also makes the material more meaningful.

4. **Reciting**. When you finish reading each section, pause to see if you've found the answers to your questions. If not, look through the section again. Sometimes you might find that the section didn't provide the information you expected. Then you need to make a new important question and find its answer. Remember: <u>If you don't understand material when you read it, there's no way you'll remember it an hour later, or the next day, or at test time.</u>

5. **Reviewing**. At the end of each article or chapter, review what you've read. You may do this by thinking through what you've learned, by glancing at headings, or by some other method. Ask yourself what the details of the chapter or article add up to. What main points are being made? Take time to think about how material you've read relates to other things you know. You may want to jot down some brief notes to review when test time approaches. Look over your notes, or review material, often.

The preceding steps may be adapted to meet your needs. Try to find the method that will work best for you.

FINDING THE MAIN IDEA

In order to find the main idea, you should understand the difference between *general* and *specific*. **General** means "overall; relating to a group or category." **Specific** means "particular; relating to a detail." Just as a military general commands thousands of troops, a main idea is a general statement that has specific subpoints.

To some extent these terms are relative. What is "general" in one situation is "specific" in another. For example, *mammal* is general compared to *horse*; however, *mammal* is specific compared to *animal*.

The main idea (or topic sentence) of a paragraph may be located anywhere within a paragraph. It may be at the beginning, at the end, or even in the middle. Sometimes the main idea isn't stated at all but is only implied. To find the main idea, ask yourself, What do these details add up to?

---

detail + detail + detail + detail + detail = MAIN IDEA

There are also different levels of main ideas. A paragraph has a main idea. However, a section of a chapter, including several paragraphs, has a main idea that is even more general than the main idea of an individual paragraph. The chapter has a main idea that is still more general.

Once you've identified the main idea, you're ready to see how other sentences relate to that idea. Details help to clarify or explain the main idea, perhaps making the main idea easier for you to understand and remember. Understanding the relationship between ideas is an important key to comprehension.

USING SIGNAL WORDS

Noticing signal words will help you see how ideas are related.

1. *And*, *in addition*, and *furthermore* tell you that the next information will agree with previous information.

2. *But*, *however*, *although*, and *on the contrary* indicate that the next information will *contrast* with what you just read. You make a sharp turn in your reading.

3. *First*, *second*, and *third* signal a series of similar items. They might be reasons, or they might be steps in a procedure. Words like *next*, *then*, and *after* also indicate a sequence of steps or events.

4. *For example*, *specifically*, and *namely* show that the next idea will illustrate the idea that was just presented. It's as if you're zooming in for a close-up.

5. **Pronouns** and **synonyms** will also help you to see how ideas are related.

Understanding the relationship between ideas will help you find the ideas that are most important.

VISUALIZING

To visualize means "to make a picture in the mind." Before television was invented, many people used to listen to radio dramas, each person creating his or her own version of the action. Today movies, television, and even MTV provide pictures *for* us.

Whether you're enjoying a story or learning information, creating mental pictures when you listen or read will bring the words to life for you. Ideas will be easier to remember if you're visualizing rather than simply manipulating words.

As you visualize, feel free to add details that the text doesn't supply. For example, make a mental picture from the following sentence.

Sam bought peanuts from the vendor at the baseball game.

Do you picture Sam and the vendor as male or female? How old are they? Does the vendor work at a concession stand or walk up and down the aisles of the stadium? Is the game, in fact, a major league game or a little league game? What is the weather—sunny, hot, overcast, raining? Does the vendor seem to enjoy selling peanuts? How is this vendor different from other vendors?

As you add details, be careful that your picture doesn't contradict anything the text told you. For example, if, after reading the boldface sentence, you pictured a basketball game, you would have ignored or changed information you'd been given. Similarly, if you later get information that doesn't fit with your picture, you need to be willing to revise your thinking. If, for example, you pictured a hot, sunny day and later learn that it's raining, you need to revisualize.

When you're reading, replay this "movie in your mind" frequently. Read and replay important sections carefully to be sure you have the correct picture. Then replay those sections so that you'll remember the image. Consider how many times an amazing or controversial play in a sports contest might be replayed on television. Each time you see it, you fix it more firmly in your mind so that you could more vividly describe it. That's what you're doing as you replay pictures of what you're reading. You're fixing the material in your mind so that you'll remember it.

OUTLINING

An outline helps you to see the relationship between ideas. It can be useful for taking notes from your reading, for taking notes from a lecture, or for organizing a composition you plan to write.

The main ideas in an outline are indicated by roman numerals. Points supporting main ideas are indented and are indicated by capital letters. Details supporting these subpoints are further indented and are indicated by arabic numerals. Minor details are indented still further and are indicated by lowercase letters. You can make a more detailed outline by using parentheses and brackets and by alternating numbers and letters. Such a detailed outline is seldom practical, however.

Parallel points in an outline are subdivisions of the preceding more important point. Since nothing can be divided into only one part, you should never have only one subdivision. Thus, if a subpoint has a *1*, it should also have a *2*; if a detail has an *a*, it should also have a *b*.

Although your outlines will not be this long, knowing **roman numerals** will help you recognize them in other situations.

I = 1	X = 10	C = 100	M = 1,000	$\overline{X}$ = 10,000	$\overline{C}$ = 100,000
V = 5	L = 50	D = 500	$\overline{V}$ = 5,000	$\overline{L}$ = 50,000	$\overline{M}$ = 1,000,000

Generally, letters with larger value are at the left and letters with smaller value are at the right. (Numbers with a 4 or a 9 are exceptions to this.) V, L, or D is never repeated in succession, and no more than three I's, X's, or C's are ever used together. When used to the right of a letter with a larger value, a letter indicates an amount *added*. When shown to the *left* of a symbol with a larger value, an I, an X, or a C indicates an amount to be *subtracted*. A horizontal line above a letter indicates that its value is multiplied by 1,000.

III = 3	IX = 9	XXXIV = 34	LX = 60
IV = 4	XI = 11	XXXIX = 39	XC = 90
VI = 6	XIX = 19	XL = 40	CD = 400
VIII = 8	XXX = 30	XLIX = 49	MCMXCIX = 1999

The sample outline on the next page shows outline form with proper subordination. It includes the same material as the discussion of the writing process on pages 132 through 136. Comparing the outline with the explanation will show you how you can outline what you read or how you can use an outline to plan what you'll write.

THE WRITING PROCESS

I. Pre-writing
   A. Define your task
      1. Choose your topic
      2. Know your audience
      3. Know your purpose
   B. Plan
      1. Jot down your ideas
      2. Determine your order

II. Writing the first draft
   A. Get your ideas down quickly without worrying about mechanics
   B. Write on only one side of the page
   C. Skip lines

III. Polishing
   A. Evaluate your own work
      1. Is your composition complete?
      2. Is your composition clear?
      3. Have you sufficiently supported your ideas?
      4. Have you created vivid pictures for the reader?
      5. Is everything geared toward your purpose?
      6. Will your lead gain the reader's attention?
      7. Will your conclusion leave the desired impression?
      8. Do sentences sound smooth?
   B. Confer—Focus on content
      1. Read your composition aloud to someone else
      2. Ask listener to "tell back" what was heard
      3. Ask which parts work well
      4. Ask for suggestions
      5. Ask open-ended questions
      6. Encourage feedback
   C. Revise
      1. Consider all suggestions
      2. Make improvements
   D. Edit—Check one thing at a time
      1. Complete sentences
      2. Paragraphing
      3. Usage
      4. Capitalization
      5. Punctuation
      6. Spelling
      7. Reread as long as you're making changes

IV. Making your final copy
   A. Allow margins
   B. Make copy neat
   C. Proofread by repeating editing steps (III-D above)

V. Sharing your ideas

WRITING

Writing is a very complex process because your brain must tend to many different things at once: you must form your idea, put it into words, think about how to spell those words, consider what to capitalize and how to punctuate, *and* remember how to form letters (or find them on a keyboard). In addition, while you're writing one sentence, your mind is likely racing ahead to what you'll say in the *next* sentence!

Although detailed instruction in writing is beyond the scope of this book, a few suggestions are offered along with models that might answer some of your questions about particular kinds of writing.

THE WRITING PROCESS

One way to make writing easier is to break the process into parts so that you can focus on each step individually. <u>At any time, even when you're trying to decide what you'll write about, you might find it helpful to talk about your ideas with someone else.</u>

1. Clarify your writing task. Choose a topic that is specific enough that you can deal with it thoroughly in the space and time available to you. Be sure you know whom you're writing for and why. Don't think of your **audience** merely as your teacher. It would be good if your writing would be read by others—classmates, perhaps, or readers of a school newspaper. Even if your teacher is the main person who'll see your work, imagine that you're writing for a specific, perhaps broader, audience—your peers, younger students, a famous author, a relative. Also have the **purpose** of your writing clearly in mind. What do you want your writing to accomplish? What response do you want from your readers?

2. Once you've determined your audience and purpose, spend some time jotting down ideas and **planning** your writing—whether you're writing a story, a poem, a report, an essay, or something else. How will you accom-

plish your purpose? Your ideas might be in the form of an outline or a web, or they might just be scattered randomly on a page. The important thing is to record them somewhere so you don't have to worry about forgetting them. That frees your mind for writing.

Write down anything you might possibly want to include. You want to develop your narrowed topic as completely as possible. For example, if you were trying to persuade someone to do something, you'd want to use the *best* arguments or those that address various aspects of the subject, not just the first ones that occur to you.

As you talk with others about what you'll write, try to choose people who'll ask questions and encourage you to talk about your topic. Your conferees don't need to be experts on your topic. In fact, people who aren't familiar with your topic might be better able to help you find ways to explain it clearly. As you talk about your topic, you'll use words that you'll later use in your writing. Talking provides an excellent rehearsal for writing.

3. Once you've gathered your ideas and put them in order, write your **first draft** as quickly as possible. Don't worry about wording, spelling, or other mechanics. Record your ideas on paper, on a computer disk, or even on magnetic tape. If you're working on a computer, <u>save your work often</u> and create one or more back-up files on different disks. If you're writing by hand, <u>write on only one side of your paper</u>. If you later decide to reorganize your composition, you'll be able to see the whole thing at once. You can even cut and paste if you want to. Obviously that's impossible if you've written on front and back. Skipping lines also simplifies revision. The important thing is to record your ideas.

If you did thorough planning, you might find that writing your first draft is simply a matter of writing a few sentences about each point in your plan. If you have trouble, though, remember that you don't need to write your composition in order. Often the introduction is one of the hardest parts to write. If you're stuck on the introduction, skip to whatever part you *do* feel ready to write. After you've written parts of your composition—or even all of it—the introduction might be easier for you to write.

4.  Once you have your ideas down, begin **polishing**. First consider *what* you're saying. Have you made your message clear? Have you adequately supported your ideas? Have you created vivid pictures that will bring your ideas to life? Is everything directed toward your purpose? Will your beginning get your readers' attention? Will your ending leave them with the thoughts and feelings you want them to have? Read your composition aloud, checking for smooth sentences.

5. Although you may have been **conferring** with others throughout the writing process, it's especially important to get feedback when you yourself are satisfied with your composition. Read your writing aloud, asking your listener to focus on the *content*, or message. Have your listener  "tell back" what he or she heard. That lets you know how your piece comes across to someone else. Ask your listener what works well in your writing, and invite suggestions for improvement. That response will be much more helpful than just saying your writing is great as it is.

If your listener is reluctant to give specific feedback, ask questions. If you're unsure of a particular section, call it to your listener's attention. Open-ended questions, rather than the yes-no variety, will give more information. For example, the answer to "What did this section mean to you?" is more helpful than the answer to "Was this part clear?" The part might have been perfectly clear to your listener, but the message received might have been quite different from the message you intended. Your attitude toward your listener's comments has a big effect on the kind of feedback you receive. If you become defensive whenever a suggestion is given, your conferee is likely to stop giving feedback. If, however, you show that you appreciate this feedback, you'll probably get more.

6. Of course, it's *your* composition; you have the final say about which changes will be made and which things will remain as they are. However, you should at least **consider suggestions**. Although your ideas may be perfectly clear to you, they might not be clear to your reader. People with whom you confer let you know how effectively your ideas come across *from your paper*. Their help is invaluable.

7. Once you're again satisfied with the content of your writing, you're ready to begin **editing**, focusing on the mechanics. You might have done some of this in your earlier polishing, but now you're editing in detail. Again it's helpful to focus on only one task at a time. Becoming familiar with your own strengths and weaknesses will help you know which editing tasks require more focused attention.

When you're editing, you need to be careful to read what's on the page, not what you *intended* to put on the page. Reading aloud slowly and pointing to one word at a time can help you with this.

a. First consider whether all of your **sentences** are complete.

b. Then see whether you have started new **paragraphs** in appropriate places. You should start a new paragraph when you move on to a new topic or major segment of your composition. If you're writing conversation, you need to start a new paragraph whenever you change speakers.

c. Third see if you have proper **usage** (subject–verb agreement, right form of verb, correct pronoun, etc.).

d. Next check to see if your **capitalization** is correct. (If this is especially difficult for you, you might want to go through your composition once checking just for capitalization at the beginning of a sentence; then go through a second time checking for words that should be capitalized within sentences.)

e. Fifth, check **punctuation**. You might want to subdivide this step also.

f. Finally, check **spelling**. It's fine to use the feature on your word processing program that checks spelling, but don't let that be your only check. That will tell you only if your words are words; it won't tell you if they're the *right* words. Be especially careful of homophones (*their* and *there*, for example). You should also check for typographical errors, such as *they* for *the*.

As long as you're making changes, you should continue proofreading. Changing one thing, such as from singular to plural, might necessitate other changes. When you've read your composition a couple of times without making any changes, you're nearing the end of the editing process.

Consider having a skilled proofreader (a peer, sibling, or parent) read especially important papers, letters, and applications. Your teacher will let you know whether you should follow this procedure with daily assignments.

8. You're now ready to make what you hope will be your **final copy**. If you're handwriting your composition, you'll need to repeat the proofreading described in Step 7. Using a word processor simplifies correction of errors. Be sure to save your work frequently and to make one or more backup disks.

9. **Share** your ideas—via your writing—with a broader audience. Enjoy your readers' responses.

YOUR IDEA BANK

Ideas for writing topics won't always come to you when you need them. Therefore, it's helpful to collect them as they occur to you and organize them so that you can find them when you want them. Although your idea bank might take a number of forms (a spiral notebook, a card file, file folders), a looseleaf notebook has several advantages. It allows you  to categorize your ideas more easily than a spiral notebook does (where you might run out of space for a topic). It also enables you to include pages that you've printed from a computer or acquired from another source. Pages are held firmly in place, yet you can easily shift them to other places. You might even use different means for cataloguing different kinds of ideas.

What should you deposit in your idea bank? Anything that might help you in your future writing: possible topics (perhaps with a few notes for development), intriguing questions, observations or descriptions of people or nature, character sketches, conversations, your reactions to personal or public events. Keeping an idea bank not only provides you with ideas when you need them, it also sharpens your awareness of the world around you.

It's also worthwhile to collect other writing that appeals to you: figures of speech, descriptions, sentences, melodic prose, systems of organization, etc. When you find something that you especially like, analyze it to try to figure out why it appeals to you. Then try to apply those qualities to your own writing. (Don't use the other author's words.) When you copy something from another author into your idea book, be sure to include that author's name and the complete source (book and page, for example). You should include enough information so that you could easily find the quotation again. Also be sure to copy the quotation without introducing any errors—in wording, spelling, punctuation, etc.

Putting a date and place (if you're not at home) on each "deposit" will provide a context that might later help you remember more about that entry. Many of your idea bank entries will be written in complete sentences and paragraphs. As the following example shows, however, sometimes a brief note is sufficient.

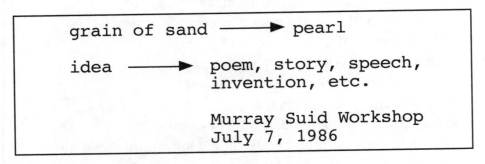

```
grain of sand ────▶ pearl

idea ────▶ poem, story, speech,
            invention, etc.

            Murray Suid Workshop
            July 7, 1986
```

PARAGRAPHS

At the beginning of this book you learned how to put words together to make a sentence. In most of your writing you'll put sentences together to make a **paragraph**, a group of sentences about one idea.

Usually a paragraph is indented—about one inch if you're writing by hand, about five spaces if you're using a word processor. Sometimes, however, block format is used, in which paragraphs begin at the left margin with a blank space between them. This book uses block format.

Where to Make Paragraph Divisions

Often there isn't just one right place to start a paragraph. In addition to being sure that all sentences relate to one idea, you should consider your reader. What divisions would be most helpful? A new paragraph signals your reader that you're moving to a slightly different aspect of your topic.

Consider the paragraphs in this section. Since all of the sentences relate to paragraphing, they could have made just one paragraph. That big chunk of type probably wouldn't have looked very inviting, and it might have been more difficult for you to read and grasp.

Understanding how ideas relate to each other will help you to paragraph effectively. Most paragraphs have general ideas and specific ideas. You might want to review the information about main ideas on page 127. Being able to identify main ideas in material you read will help you include and support main ideas when you write.

The Topic Sentence

As explained in the Reading section (page 127) most paragraphs have a topic sentence. The topic sentence may come at the beginning, the middle, or the end of a paragraph—or it may only be implied rather than stated. Putting the topic sentence at the beginning of a paragraph immediately presents the main idea so that your reader can relate details to it. Sometimes, however, you might not want to present the main idea right away. For example, if your reader might be unlikely to accept the main idea—or might even find it offensive, you might want to first present details that would help your reader to understand your point of view.

A good topic sentence doesn't just state the topic of the paragraph; it says something *about* that topic. It states a fact that will be discussed further or it asserts an opinion. Notice the following examples.

WEAK: *I'm going to tell you about my trip to Alaska.*

BETTER: *My trip to Alaska was my greatest adventure.*

As you read the example paragraphs on the following pages, notice the placement and content of the topic sentences.

Characteristics of Paragraphs

A good paragraph has both unity and coherence. **Unity** means that all sentences in a paragraph contribute to the main idea. To test a paragraph's unity, first identify the main idea. Then see if all sentences relate to that idea.

Soccer is the most popular sport in the world. It began, in a somewhat different form, more than two thousand years ago. It is now played by millions of people on six continents. Soccer's inexpensive equipment and relatively simple rules contribute to its popularity. I really like soccer. My team won the league championship last year.

[The first sentence states the main idea, that soccer is popular. The next three sentences provide support. The last two sentences, however, damage the paragraph's unity. Notice that the shift away from the main idea is gradual (as it often is). "Liking soccer" is related to the idea of the sport's popularity. The shift from third to first person indicates that the writer is veering off course.]

Coherence means that sentences in a paragraph "stick together." The specific words that are used (the transition words, repeated words, synonyms, and pronouns) help to  join one idea to the next just as pieces of a jigsaw puzzle fit together. In the following paragraph, the main words that contribute to the paragraph's coherence are **boldfaced**. You'll see that the words represent several ideas that are braided together in the paragraph.

*The **water** on our **planet** has been **recycling itself** since time began. After **rain** falls to **earth**, the **water** flows along the **ground**, where **it** might be lapped up by **animals**, or **it** soaks into the **ground**, where **it** might be absorbed by **plants**. The **water** eventually reaches a **pond**, **river**, **ocean**, or other body of **water**. Even the **water** that is taken in by **plants** or **animals** is eventually given off by **them**. As **water** on the **earth** becomes **warmer**, **it** changes to a **vapor** and becomes part of the **air**. **Water** in the **air** forms **clouds**. In upper levels of the **atmosphere**, where **temperatures** are **cooler**, the **water vapor** becomes **liquid** again (if **temperatures** are extremely **cold**, the **water** might become **ice** or **snow**). As **clouds** become heavy with **moisture**, gravity pulls the **water** to **earth**, completing the **cycle**.*

Although unity and coherence are closely related, it's possible for a paragraph to have one quality and lack the other. Notice how unity and coherence are achieved in the following paragraphs that illustrate different methods of development.

Ways to Develop a Paragraph

Some of the most common ways to organize information within a paragraph are explained and illustrated below. Considering the type of information you're presenting usually helps you decide which method of organization to use. You want to present the information so that it will be as easy as possible for your reader to understand.

Time. If you're telling about a sequence of events—a story, an incident, even a set of directions—you're likely to relate them in the order in which they happened. This is called **chronological** order (*chron* means "time"). Words signaling a time relationship are boldfaced in the example below.

> *S'mores, a special treat at a cookout, are easy to make. (They're called "s'mores" because they're so good that people always want "s'more" of them.)* **Before** *you begin, get the necessary ingredients: graham crackers, a bag of regular-size marshmallows, and flat chocolate bars (each chocolate bar will make two or three s'mores). Be sure to keep the chocolate away from excessive heat so that it won't melt. To prepare a s'more,* **first** *use a long pointed stick to roast your marshmallow* **until** *it's done just the way you like it.* **Next** *break a rectangular graham cracker into two squares.* **After this,** *place one third or one half of a chocolate bar on top of one of the squares.* **Then** *carefully slide the marshmallow off the stick and onto the chocolate.* **Finally,** *put the other graham cracker square on top of the marshmallow, pressing it down so that the marshmallow covers most of the chocolate. Enjoy!*

[Instructions, such as these, might more likely be written as numbered steps. The signal words help to make them clear, however. Using the imperative (commands) for all

141

sentences except the introductory one contributes to the coherence of the paragraph.]

Space. If you're describing a place at one moment in time, it will be easier for your reader to visualize the scene if you move logically around the area rather than jump from one spot to another. You might first describe the view from a distance, then move closer to your subject, describing details in an organized way, such as moving clockwise around a room. Notice how details are organized in this description of a person.

The man at the next table in the lunchroom had a massive head that seemed to sit directly on his broad shoulders. His face was gray-green, the same color as the sweater that stretched to button around his paunch. His dark hair—greasy, curly—had begun to recede, but wiry gray sideburns abounded. Large black-rimmed glasses, tinted gray, were amply supported by his long hook nose and large ears. His jaw maintained a circular motion— simultaneously talking and chewing—revealing crooked teeth. From his thick lips dangled a long strand of heavily sauced spaghetti.

[This paragraph begins with observations of size and color that the writer (or reader) could make from a distance. Detailed description begins at the top of the head and moves downward. Notice that this paragraph has no topic sentence. The writer presents details objectively and lets the reader draw his or her own conclusion. What would you say is the main idea of the paragraph?]

Examples or Reasons. While the content of these two methods of development is different, the principle of organization is the same. The paragraph consists of examples or reasons that support the main idea. Be sure to consider the best order for your examples or reasons. Which information should logically precede other information? How will you achieve coherence? Could some information be organized according to time or space?

142

The most violent explosion in the history of the earth occurred on August 27, 1883, on the island of Krakatoa in the South China Sea. The energy released from the volcanic eruption was equivalent to 200 megatons of TNT. The explosion, which was heard 3,000 miles away, blew away the northern two thirds of the island. Some debris was hurled seventeen miles into the air, creating a cloud of dust and ash that circled the earth for a year. The explosion also created huge tidal waves that killed more than 36,000 people—some from the torrents of water, some from the 600-ton blocks of coral that washed ashore.

Comparison or Contrast.

Comparison focuses on similarities between things; contrast focuses on differences. There are two basic ways to organize comparison/contrast paragraphs. One way is to organize by points of comparison, discussing each item in relation to each point. The boldfaced words in the example below highlight that organization.

*Although a frog and a toad have many similarities, there are several simple ways to tell them apart. First is **habitat**. A **frog** usually lives in or near water; a **toad** spends most of its time on land. A second important difference is **skin**. A **frog**'s skin is moist and slimy (and has no warts). A **toad**'s skin is dry and bumpy. A final major difference is **hind feet and legs**. A **frog** has long, strong legs and webbed feet, making it well adapted to leaping and swimming. A **toad** has short hind legs and is likely to walk instead of hop.*

[The characteristics of comparison are arranged in the order that you're likely to notice them. Consistently describing the frog's characteristics first makes the comparison easier to follow.]

143

The other way to organize a paragraph of comparison is to present all information about one item and then present all information about the other item. Notice how information in the previous example could be rearranged.

> *Do you have trouble distinguishing a frog from a toad? A **frog** lives in or near water. It has moist, slimy skin, and its long, strong hind legs and webbed hind feet are designed for leaping and swimming. A **toad**, **on the other hand**, lives mainly on land. Its skin is dry and bumpy, and its short hind legs are adapted for walking.*

[The transition phrase "on the other hand" signals the beginning of the second part of the comparison.]

To decide which method of comparison will work best in each situation, consider your reader and the information you're presenting.

Definition. Sometimes you'll want to spend an entire paragraph—or even an entire composition—defining a term. You'd probably begin with a sentence definition in standard form, putting the item into a class and then distinguishing it from other items in that class. In your extended definition you might clarify the term by means of examples. You might say what the term is *not*. You might compare the term with some things or contrast it with others.

> *Poetry is writing that is not prose. Instead of being written in paragraphs as prose is, poetry is written with definite line breaks. Sometimes a line has a particular rhythm or rhyme; sometimes it does not. Occasionally a line of poetry forms part of a picture on a page. Poetry is known for its description, its musical quality, and its effective word choices. However, prose sometimes has those qualities as well. The main difference between poetry and prose is that poetry has definite line breaks.*

[Not only does *poetry* have several definitions, it's a term that's quite subjective; people have different ideas about what makes poetry and what does not. In evaluating this as a paragraph, consider whether the viewpoint has been presented clearly. Notice that the distinguishing characteristic of poetry has been repeated in the last sentence.]

Cause and Effect. This type of paragraph establishes a relationship between two events. It may, in fact, lead the reader through a series of events that links the cause with the effect. The paragraph may move in either direction—from cause to effect, or from effect to cause.

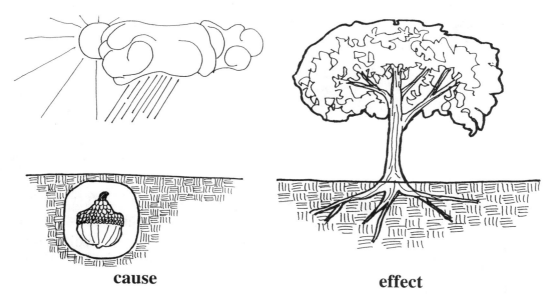

cause   **effect**

Grasses do not survive on the North American prairie as well as they did centuries ago. The root system of the native grasses went about thirty feet deep, allowing the grasses to find and hold the moisture they needed, even in times of drought. Today, however, many of the native grasses have been replaced by grasses that originated in Europe, where the annual rainfall is lower than in the central United States. Although these plants are accustomed to less moisture than they now receive, their shallow root system makes it more difficult for them to find and store water. They have difficulty, therefore, surviving a drought.

Many paragraphs combine several methods in their development. Although the previous example begins with an effect and eventually explains its cause, it also includes comparison and contrast.

145

COMPOSITIONS

Composition, in the broad sense, can refer to any piece of original writing. Once you can write a paragraph, you can use those same skills to write a longer composition (a series of paragraphs). You'll begin with the first steps of the writing process (page 132). Once you've narrowed your topic and determined your purpose, you'll decide what to include and in what order you want to present your information. You may apply many of the principles discussed in the preceding section. For example, your entire composition might be a chronological account or a comparison.

Certain paragraphs in your composition, such as the opening paragraph and the concluding paragraph, deserve special attention.

The Opening Paragraph

The first paragraph must capture your reader's attention. When you're a student, your teacher is generally obligated to read what you write. In the "real world," however, your reader has no such duty. If you can't keep your reader interested, he or she will set your message aside; you will have lost the opportunity to get your point across.

There are a number of ways to capture attention: an intriguing question, a startling fact, a gripping anecdote, an appropriate quotation. Of course, the opening paragraph must also provide a suitable introduction to your topic, perhaps stating the main idea of your composition or providing relevant background information.

The Concluding Paragraph

As you write your concluding paragraph, remember that it will determine your reader's final impression. Ask yourself (again) what you want your reader to know or feel or do when he or she finishes reading your message. Then be sure that your words will convey the information, evoke the feeling, or spur to action. The concluding paragraph often includes a restatement of the composition's main idea.

Throughout the Composition

You need to maintain certain consistencies throughout your composition. Your point of view should be consistent. If you're using first person (*I*), you should do so consistently rather than shift back and forth between first person and third. You should also maintain a consistent level of seriousness (or lightheartedness) and formality (or informality). Tense (time) should be consistent, too. For example, if you're recounting a story, you should decide whether you'll use past tense or present tense. Of course, if you're talking about *different* times, different tenses are appropriate.

PROOFREADER'S MARKS

Writers, editors, and typesetters use standardized proofreading symbols. If you begin using these symbols now, you'll be learning a "language" that will enable you to communicate with many other people.

¶   This symbol marks the beginning of a **paragraph**. It should be placed exactly where the paragraph is to begin, not just in the margin.

≡   Three lines under one or more letters show that they are to be **capitalized**.

/   A slanted line going through a letter at this angle indicates that the letter is to be **lowercased**. If consecutive capitalized letters are to be lowercased, this line would go through the first letter and a horizontal line would extend from the top of this line above all letters to the right.

∧   This symbol, called a **caret**, indicates where one or more letters or words should be **inserted**. (When a comma is inserted, a caret is usually placed above it so that it's more easily seen.) The inserted word or letter should be written *above* the line to which it's to be added. If there isn't enough space above the line, find a place where there *is* space. If that is elsewhere on the page, neatly draw a line around the material to be inserted, and join it to the caret. If the material to be inserted must be written on a separate page, clearly label it *Insert 1*, *Insert A*, etc., and put a corresponding label at the point where the insertion is to be made.

This "upside-down caret" is used for **insertions** that would be **above the regular line of type**, such as apostrophes, quotation marks, and superior numerals for footnotes. The symbol to be added is written in the "v" of the caret.

Commonly called the **delete** symbol, this mark indicates that one or more words, letters, or punctuation marks are to be **taken out**.

This symbol, which means to **close up space**, is often used with the delete symbol. After something has been deleted, the space created needs to be closed. This symbol means to close space entirely. Using only the top part of the symbol means to close space partially, usually leaving space between remaining words.

This versatile symbol has several meanings. In editing it's used to show where **space** is to be inserted between words or between lines.

When a **period** is inserted, a circle is put around it so it's more easily seen.

As the curving of this symbol suggests, it indicates that letters or words are to be **transposed** (shifted so that their order is reversed).

┌─   This symbol would be placed at the point where a **new line** should start. You might use it when writing poetry, a quotation, a list, or something else that you want to set off.

|| Two parallel vertical lines indicate that two lines should be **aligned** or indented the same amount. This might be used to mark the heading of a letter.

Notice how these symbols are used to show editing changes in the following paragraph.

¶ Reading and experience can ⌐sometimes⌐ be blended in such a way that each ~~is rich~~ _enriches the other_ ~~er for their union~~. For example, Ray Bradbury's <u>Dandelion Wine</u> is most effectively read in summer. Hot, humid ~~summer~~ days help the reader to experience the atmosphere of an Illinois summer. Reading about Douglas's adventures, which have aged in memory like bottles of dandelion wine in a wine cellar, helps us to become more aware of our own experiences ⊙ _in the days before air conditioning_

Sometimes teachers put symbols in the left-hand margin of a paper to indicate the kinds of corrections that are needed. Unlike the proofreader's symbols shown earlier, these symbols are not standard. They will vary from one teacher to another. Be sure to learn the system your teacher uses. Some of these symbols are shown on the next page.

sp	Look for a **misspelled word**.
cap	Look for a **capitalization error**. This might be a word that isn't capitalized and needs to be, or a word that is capitalized and shouldn't be.
P	Look for a **punctuation error**. This might be punctuation you need to add or punctuation you need to take away.
RO	Look for a **run-on sentence**. Although this is a type of punctuation error (and likely involves capitalization as well), it's such a common error that it often gets its own symbol.
frag	Look for a sentence **fragment**.
W	Look for a **wrong word**. It might be a wrong homophone (*to* for *too*, for example), a wrong verb form, or any of a number of other things.
?	Something is **unclear**. Look for writing that is illegible or ideas that don't seem to make sense.

The passage below has been marked as a teacher might mark it for student correction. Can you figure out what needs to be changed? (A diagonal line is used to separate two corrections on one line.)

cap
sp
sp / P
frag

One sure sign of Spring is the bird
that each year tries to build it's
nest in our mailbox. It announces
it's arrival with shrill calls, and
wildly flapping wings. When we
investigate. We find a collection
of twigs, dry grass, and an
assortment of other "building

```
           materials." Once we even found a
           plastic drinking straw! This is no
RO/sp      dumb bird, it has probly picked the
           best nesting spot for miles around.
           What other bird has a brick nest
  P        lined with metal.
```

FRIENDLY LETTERS

Writing letters can be a very rewarding experience. It gives you a chance to share organized and polished ideas with another person or perhaps, as in the case of a letter to a newspaper editor, with the rest of the community. For many people, the most rewarding part of letter-writing is getting a response—whether that response is a personal letter in their mailbox or a change in public policy.

Letters follow a particular format. The example on the next page shows the parts of a friendly letter. The **heading** lets your reader know when the letter was written and where a reply should be sent. You may omit your address if you're writing to someone who knows you (and your address) well.

The **closing**, also called the **complimentary close**, shows your relationship to the reader or the attitude with which you send the letter. Some appropriate closings are *Sincerely, Yours truly, Fondly, Your friend, Your pen pal,* or *Your cousin.* Neither *From* nor *Thank you* is an appropriate closing. If you want to thank your reader, you should do so in the body of your letter. The closing is followed by a comma, and only the first letter of the first word is capitalized.

The thank-you note on the next page illustrates the form of a friendly letter. It's followed by an appropriately addressed envelope.

8721 Sierra Drive
[HEADING]   St. Louis, MO 63117
April 3, 2004

[SALUTATION or
Dear Grandma and Grandpa,   **GREETING]**

B   Thanks for the beautiful pink sweater you sent
me for my birthday. It's my favorite color and looks
O   great with the navy slacks and print blouse I got from
Mom.
D   I can't wait to see you in the summer. I love to
have you tell me about the things Mom did with
Y   Aunt Ellie and Uncle Frank when they were kids. I'll
see you soon!

[CLOSING]   Love,

[SIGNATURE]   *Crystal*

Crystal Meyer
8721 Sierra Drive
St. Louis, MO 63117

Mr. and Mrs. Stephen Graham

2937 Pembroke Way

Memphis, TN 38129

BUSINESS LETTERS

The main difference between a business letter and a friendly letter is that a business letter relates to business (or school) matters rather than to personal matters. For that reason, and because a business letter often is written to someone with whom the writer is not acquainted, it is <u>more formal</u> than a friendly letter. Here are some guidelines for writing effective business letters.

1. Make every effort to send your letter to a **specific person** rather than use the general salutation *Dear Sir* or *To whom it may concern.* Sending your letter to a specific person often increases your chances of getting a favorable reply. If you don't know the name of the person to whom you should write, you can usually find out by telephoning the company or by checking the company's website. While you're on the phone, check the spelling of the person's name; even common names can have unusual spellings.

2. Be sure that your letter has only **one purpose**. Everything in your letter should be geared toward getting a particular response. If you have two purposes, you should send two letters. Trying to accomplish both purposes in one letter will cut your effectiveness in half.

| refund | order | job | sale | info |

3. Keep your letter **short**. Short paragraphs will make it easier for your busy reader to identify your main points. Some paragraphs in your letter might have only one sentence.

4. Make yourself **clear**. Directly (but politely) state exactly what you would like the reader to do. You're more likely to get what you want if the reader doesn't have to read your mind.

5. Most business transactions benefit both parties: When a customer makes a purchase, a business makes a sale; when a person applies for

a job, a company may get a valuable employee. However, if your letter requests a favor and the person or business will receive no direct benefit, you should enclose a self-addressed stamped envelope (**SASE**). It greatly increases the possibility of your receiving a prompt reply. SASEs are often appropriate for letters requesting information. The writer of the example business letter on page 155 did not enclose one because he was writing to a Chamber of Commerce. His project on Portland would help the Chamber of Commerce achieve its goal of publicizing the city.

6. Write the letter neatly in **standard form**. Although a format similar to that used for the friendly letter on page 152 looks more balanced, most letters are written in **block format** (in which each line starts at the left-hand margin). Block format is shown in the example on page 155.

In addition to the parts of a friendly letter, a business letter contains an **inside address**. That includes the <u>name and address of the person to whom you're writing</u>. It's identical to the main address on the envelope. The inside address helps the letter get to the right person, even when the letter is separated from the envelope.

Dear in the salutation may seem overly affectionate for a business letter. However, it's just a formality. Use the person's name as you would if you were speaking to him or her. Usually you'd use a title and a last name, such as *Ms. MacLean* or *Dr. Chin*. If you can't tell from the first name whether the person is a man or a woman, it's fine to use both names—for example, *Dear Leslie Russell*. <u>Notice that the salutation is followed by a colon rather than a comma</u> as in the friendly letter. This is part of the letter's formality.

Sincerely or *Yours truly* is a good closing for a business letter. As in the friendly letter, the closing is followed by a comma, and only the first letter of the first word is capitalized. If your business letter is typed, your name should be typed four spaces below the closing. That ensures that the reader will be able to read your name. You should sign your name (in cursive) in the space below the closing.

The preceding points about a business letter—its content as well as its form—are illustrated in the example on the next page.

154

9847 Sheridan Lake Road
Rapid City, SD 57718   [HEADING]
September 22, 2003

Ms. Diane Larsen, Director
Portland Chamber of Commerce   [INSIDE
221 NW 2nd Avenue   ADDRESS]
Portland, OR 97209

Dear Ms. Larsen: [SALUTATION or GREETING]

B The theme for my school's social studies fair this year is "River Cities." I have chosen to do my project on Portland.

O Please send me information related to this topic. I am especially interested in how the river contributed to Portland's population growth and how the river is important to the city's major industries. Are the

D industries that were responsible for Portland's early growth still important today?

Y I would appreciate receiving this information as soon as possible since I am eager to get an early start on my project. Thank you very much for your help.

Yours truly,   [CLOSING]

Brian Jensen

Brian Jensen   [SIGNATURE]

FOLDING A LETTER

Once you've written your letter, you need to get it neatly into its addressed envelope. The edges of the paper should align after the paper is folded, and the thickness of the letter should be uniform; one side should not be bulkier than the other.

Believe it or not, a letter on 8 1/2- by 11-inch paper can fit neatly into an envelope that is either 4 1/8 inches by 9 1/2 inches, or 3 5/8 inches by 6 1/2 inches (or variations thereof). Folding for the longer envelope is one step shorter. (Some letters that come to your home may be folded differently from this because they may have been folded for a window envelope or folded by machine. This is still the method you should use.) Basically, you are making two folds to fold your letter approximately into thirds.

1. Lay the envelope with the address side down and the flap up.

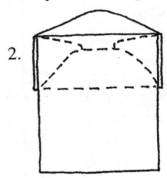

2. Put the top of your letter face up under the flap so that the top of the paper is against the fold. Be sure the paper is against the fold *all the way across*.

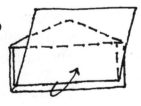

3. Move the bottom of the letter up beyond the top of the envelope so that you can see about 1/4 inch of the envelope below the letter. <u>Be sure the sides of the letter align.</u> Crease.

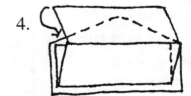

4. Move the bottom of the letter toward the inside of the crease you just made. About 1/4 inch should be showing at the top of the letter. Again align the sides of your letter. Crease.

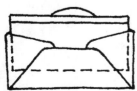

5. Put the letter into the envelope so that the top of the letter is at the top of the envelope. This will be convenient for the person who opens the letter.

Letters on 8 1/2- by 11-inch paper often look very messy when they come out of 3 5/8- by 6 1/2-inch envelopes. They needn't. You'll be making three folds for this letter. The first two steps are identical to folding for the long envelope.

1. Lay the envelope with the address side down and the flap up.

2. Put the top of your letter face up under the flap so that the top of the paper is against the fold. Be sure the paper is against the fold *all the way across.*

3. 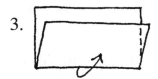 Place the bottom edge of the letter about 1/4 inch below the top edge of the letter. Align the sides of your letter. Crease.

4. With the letter folded nearly in half, move the left side of the letter so that it's about 3 inches from the right edge of the letter. Align the edges. Crease.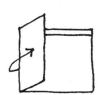

5. 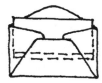 Maintaining these two folds, move the right edge of the letter toward the left so that the right edge of the letter is about 1/2 inch from the fold you just made. Again align the edges. Crease.

6. Slip the letter into the envelope so that the top of the letter is toward the left.

MAKING A BIBLIOGRAPHY

A **bibliography** is a list of references used in preparing a project or report. Two main purposes of a bibliography are to give credit to your sources and to tell readers where they can double-check your information or learn more about your topic. Be sure that information in your bibliography is <u>accurate</u> and as <u>complete</u> as possible.

As soon as you realize that a source contains information that you might use in your report, you should take down that source's bibliographic data. It will be much more efficient to get the information immediately than to risk having to try to find the source again, perhaps after you have returned it to a library.

The information given about each source makes up a **bibliography entry**. Entries should be arranged in <u>alphabetical order</u> according to their first letter. They should *not* <u>be numbered</u>. <u>Runover lines</u> within an entry should be <u>indented</u>. The entire bibliography should be <u>double-spaced</u>. The preferred title for this page, which usually appears at the end of your report, is Works Cited (rather than Bibliography). That title emphasizes that these are sources you really used, not just sources that have information on your topic.

There are several correct ways to arrange information within a bibliography entry. You should consistently follow one of the accepted styles. The examples below follow the style recommended by the Modern Language Association (MLA). This style is used for most general writing. Other styles may be recommended in specialized fields.

After studying these examples, you'll probably be able to figure out how to make an appropriate entry for a different type of source. You could also consult a reference book that gives more detailed information about writing research papers.

The parts of each entry are first listed with appropriate punctuation between them. Then an example of that type of entry is given. Although punctuation marks are emphasized here, you should use regular text type for your punctuation. MLA style calls for underlining titles even though italic type may be available. <u>Whenever a piece of information in a bibliography entry (such as an author or a city) is not available, just skip it and go on to the next piece of information.</u>

Book With One Author

Author (last name first). <u>Title</u>. City: Publisher, Publication Date.

Lederer, Richard. <u>The Miracle of Language</u>. New York: Pocket Books, 1991.

The publisher is usually found near the bottom of the title page. If more than one city is listed there, choose the one closest to you. The date is usually found on the back of the title page. Sometimes more than one date is listed. Use the original date unless the work has been revised. In the case of a revision, use the original date after the title and the date of the revision you're using at the end of the entry.

Book with Two Authors

Mellonie, Bryan, and Robert Ingpen. <u>Lifetimes: A Beautiful Way to Explain Death to Children</u>. New York: Bantam Books, 1983.

Notice that the first name of the second author precedes the last name.

Encyclopedia Entry

"Entry," <u>Title of Encyclopedia</u>, edition.

"Acupuncture," <u>The World Book Encyclopedia</u>, 2003 ed.

Magazine Article

Author (last name first). "Article Title." <u>Magazine Title</u>. Date (day Month year): pages.

Ridley, Matt. "What Makes You Who You Are." <u>Time</u>. 2 June 2003: 54–63.

All months except May, June, and July should be abbreviated. (This holds true for any kind of entry that includes a month.) If pages of the article are not consecutive, give only the number of the first page followed by **+**, without intervening space (example: 54+).

Personal Interview

Name. Personal interview. Date (day Month year).

Chang, Cheryl. Personal interview. 6 Oct. 2003.

Television Program

"Title of Episode." <u>Title of Program</u>. Title of Series (if applicable). Name of network. Call letters, City of local station. Broadcast date (day Month year).

<u>The FBI</u>. National Geographic Special. PBS. KETC, St. Louis. 23 July 2003.

Since this program was a special, it did not have an episode title. Many programs will have only two of the three titles mentioned in the parts of the entry above.

Portable Database (CD-ROM, Diskette, Magnetic Tape, etc.)

Author (if available). "Title of article, entry, story, poem, etc." <u>Title of Product</u>. Edition, release, or version. Medium. City of Publication: Publisher, Date.

Garst, Ronald D. "Kenya." <u>Grolier Multimedia Encyclopedia</u>. Version 7.0.2. CD-ROM. Grolier Electronic Publishing, Inc., 1995.

Note that a city was not available for this entry.

Online Sources: E-mail

Author. <Author's e-mail address>. "Subject line of message." Personal e-mail. Date (day Month year).

Green, Cindy. <cgreen56@aol.com>. "Family History." Personal e-mail. 14 Apr. 2003.

Double-check the accuracy of e-mail addresses or URL (Uniform Resource Locator) addresses. Enclosing an online address in angular brackets will help to separate it from the rest of the entry. Be sure that any punctuation following the address is *outside* the closing bracket so that it doesn't look like part of the address.

Online Sources: Website

Author. "Title of Article." Name of Website. Group or Organization Responsible for Publishing Information. Date of publication or last revision. <URL>. Date of access (day Month year).

Lynds, Beverly T. "About Rainbows." Unidata. 19 Sept. 1995. <http://www.unidata.ucar.edu/staff/blynds/rnbw.html>. 5 Apr. 2004.

Many websites will not have articles and will not identify their authors. As with other sources, you should begin your entry with the first piece of information that you have. If your information is from an electronic version of material (such as a magazine) that also appears in print, the first part of your entry should be a bibliography entry for the print version. Immediately follow that, on the same line, with the information specified above. _Date of access_ for online sources is especially important since the materials, unlike books, may be changed frequently. If part of an electronic address must appear on another line, the address should be broken only at a slash, a period, or a hyphen.

FOOTNOTES

There are two kinds of footnotes. **Content footnotes** give helpful information that might be too interruptive if included in the body of your report. Definitions are examples of content footnotes. Content footnotes should be used sparingly because they can distract and annoy the reader. Before you write a footnote, ask yourself whether the information is important. If you decide that it is, consider whether you should include it in the body of your report rather than in a footnote. You can find examples of content footnotes in this book at the bottom of the irregular verb charts on pages 40 and 41.

The second kind of footnote is a **reference footnote**. While a bibliography lists a researcher's sources, reference footnotes tell which information came from which source. Any source you cite in a footnote should also be included in your bibliography.

Inexperienced researchers often wonder which material they need to footnote. If you use someone else's exact words, you need to put those words in quotation marks and indicate your source. (You should always put ideas into your own words unless the original author's exact wording is necessary.) There are many times, however, when you should give credit for an *idea* even though you're using your own *words*. Generally, unless information is a commonly known fact, a commonly shared opinion, or your original idea, you should indicate your source. Citing an authority supports your point.

Footnotes are much simpler to use than they used to be. They used to be placed at the bottom of the page containing the information to which they referred (hence, the name *foot*notes). This often created a nightmare for typists. Today footnotes, usually called *end*notes, may appear at the end of the entire paper instead of at the bottom of each page. They should start on a new page, titled *Notes*, and should be numbered consecutively throughout your report. On the Notes page, the number of the note should be slightly above the line (as it is in the report itself). It should be followed by a space but no punctuation. Endnotes should be double-spaced.

Footnotes used to include the same information as bibliography entries. However, the information was arranged a little differently. Here is an example of the long form for a footnote.

[1] Richard Lederer, The Miracle of Language (New York: Pocket Books, 1991) 19.

The number at the end is a page number (page numbers of books do not appear in a bibliography). If you study this example and compare it with the bibliography entry for the same source on page 158, you'll have a guideline for converting your bibliography entries to footnotes.

Today, rather than appearing at the bottom of the page or at the end of the report, "footnotes" are often included in parentheses within the body of the report. This is easier for both the writer and the reader. The notes identify the source of the information with little interruption of the text. Include a page number and only enough information to identify the source in your bibliography. Notice various short forms for the note cited earlier.

(Lederer 19) (This most common form would follow Mr. Lederer's idea in the body of the report.)

(19) (Only the page number would be used if Mr. Lederer's name had been included in the body of the report in relation to the cited material.)

(R. Lederer 19) (If your bibliography includes works by more than one author named *Lederer*, you'd use the initial to identify the one you mean.)

(Lederer, *Miracle* 19) (If your bibliography includes two works by Lederer, you'd use a shortened form of the title to indicate the source you're citing.)

Even more important than using proper *form* for footnotes is giving credit where it's due. Passing off someone else's ideas as your own is called **plagiarism**. It's against the law. Students are sometimes expelled from schools for plagiarism.

ACTIVE AND PASSIVE VOICE

As you write more (and read more), you'll probably want to become an even better writer. One way to make your writing livelier and more direct is to use **active voice**. In active voice the subject of the sentence performs an action.

Amy scored *a goal.*

In **passive voice** the subject is acted upon by some other agent.

*A **goal was scored** by Amy.*

*A **goal was scored**.*

If the person or thing performing the action is indicated, it will be in a prepositional phrase beginning with *by*. The doer of the action has less importance than in active voice when it is the subject of the sentence. In passive voice the verb will always be *at least* two words (a form of "to be" plus a past participle). Passive voice, therefore, requires more words than active voice does.

<u>Passive voice may occur in past, present, or future tense.</u>

*Dinner **was cooked** by Dad.* [passive voice; past tense]

*Dad **cooked** dinner.* [active voice; past tense]

*Most of our milk **is produced** by cows.* [passive; present]

*Cows **produce** most of our milk.* [active; present]

*Snacks **will be brought** by the sixth graders.* [passive; future]

*The sixth graders **will bring** snacks.* [active; future]

<u>Usually it's better to use active voice in your writing.</u> It's shorter, livelier, and more direct. Sometimes, however, passive voice is better.

*The bank **was robbed**.* [The doer of the action is unknown.]

*The temperature **was varied**.* [The action is more important than the person or thing performing it. A report of a science experiment is one situation in which passive voice is preferable.]

164

CONCISENESS

The *cise* root in *conciseness* means "cut." It's the same root you see in *incision*. When you make your writing concise, you're cutting out unnecessary words. Making your writing concise doesn't mean that you're making your writing sound like a telegram, with small connecting words omitted. Neither does it mean that you're eliminating description that adds vividness—or omitting repetition that creates an emotional impact.

You may have learned in math that "the shortest distance between two points is a straight line." Conciseness applies this principle to your writing. Think about it: When fewer words say the same thing, the words are more powerful.

In the section above, you learned that active voice is more direct than passive voice and uses fewer words. Using **active voice**, then, is one way to make your writing more concise. Here are some others.

Eliminate Repetitive Expressions

Each of the following phrases contains two words with the same meaning. Such expressions are said to be **redundant**. Eliminating redundancies is one of the easiest ways to improve conciseness.

the exact same thing	close proximity
all throughout	consensus of opinion
throughout the entire	basic fundamentals
sum total	originally began
a.m. in the morning	refer back
true facts	cooperate together
past experience	round in shape
future plans	blue in color
free gift	five in number
completely surrounded	the state of California

This sample of repetitive expressions should begin to make you aware of the kinds of phrases to shorten.

Use Simple, Direct Language

Another way to improve conciseness is to use simple, direct language:

Wordy	Concise
at this point in time	now
at the earliest possible moment	soon
in order that	so
in the event that	if
in the neighborhood of	about
in the amount of	for
in the normal course of procedure	normally
in view of the fact that	since
despite the fact that	although
we are not in a position to	we cannot
will you be kind enough to	please
we are cognizant of the fact that	we know
this letter is for the purpose of	(omit; get to the point)

These are just a few examples of the many weighty expressions that have crept into our language. Simplify them—and others like them.

Make the Subject and Verb the Core of Your Sentence

You'll be well on the way to writing a concise sentence if the subject and verb of your independent clause include the main idea of your sentence. Notice these examples:

WORDY: *It is essential that we follow these procedures if our workers are to be safe.*

CONCISE: *We must follow these procedures for our workers' safety.*

In addition to including more words, the first sentence has three clauses; the second has just one. The subject and verb of the second sentence come much closer to conveying the main idea of the sentence than do the subject and verb of the independent clause of the first sentence (*It is*).

Be Positive Rather Than Negative

It's usually more effective—and shorter—to tell what something *is* rather than what it is *not*.

> NEGATIVE: *She did not pay attention to the warning.*
>
> POSITIVE: *She ignored the warning.*

> NEGATIVE: *He doesn't do anything to help me.*
>
> POSITIVE: *He does nothing to help me.*

Although the "positive" sentence in the second pair above contains a negative word (*nothing*), the sentence tells what the person *does* rather than what he *doesn't* do. Two forms of *do* in the first sentence of that pair signal that the sentence can be tightened.

Avoid Qualifiers

One kind of **qualifier** is a word, such as *very* or *somewhat*, that modifies an adjective or adverb. When you use a qualifier, you often miss an opportunity to use a more vivid descriptive word.

Qualified	Vivid
very surprised	astonished
very angry	furious
very stubborn	obstinate
very weak	frail

Another kind of qualifier uses words that weaken the original statement.

> QUALIFIED: *I think this book would probably be a great resource for you.*
>
> DIRECT: *This book will be a great resource for you.*

In the first sentence, *think*, *would*, and *probably* weaken the recommendation. In addition, the subject and verb of the independent clause of the first sentence are "I think"—not the core of the sentence. The first sentence buries the most important information in a dependent clause. Such qualified statements can help a person to be tactful or can soften bad news.

Use Specific Verbs

Since verbs are such an important part of a sentence, making them as specific as possible eliminates the need for additional explanation.

WORDY: *I fastened the papers with a staple.*

CONCISE: *I stapled the papers.*

Although *fastened* is a good word, *stapled* is even more specific and eliminates the need for a prepositional phrase.

Avoid Using Forms of "To Be"

Forms of "to be" (*is, am, are, was, were*, etc.) are so frequently used that totally eliminating them would be impossible. Think twice about them though. They are so bland that they rely on additional words to make a sentence meaningful. Especially try to avoid beginning a sentence with *there is* or *there are*.

WORDY: *There are some children who need extra attention.*

CONCISE: *Some children need extra attention.*

Again, construction is simpler; a dependent clause has been eliminated.

SENTENCE VARIETY

Your writing will be more interesting and more effective if you vary the length and pattern of your sentences. When you read or hear a sentence with an interesting structure, add it to your idea bank so that you can use that structure in your own writing.

In addition to the discussion of sentences on pages 16 to 30, the following examples show some ways to vary your sentences. Numbers in brackets indicate pages where you can find additional information.

1. Write an interrogative sentence (a question). [page 24]

   Why can't the world's problems hit us at eighteen, when we know everything? (Anonymous)

2. Write an imperative sentence (a command). [page 24]

   Learn as much by writing as by reading. (Lord Acton, English historian, 1834–1902)

3. Write an exclamatory sentence. [page 24]

   How many good books suffer neglect through the inefficiency of their beginnings! (Edgar Allan Poe, U.S. writer, 1809–1849)

4. Write a direct quotation. [pages 85–87]

   "Give me liberty, or give me death!" proclaimed Patrick Henry. (American patriot, orator, and statesman, 1736– 1799)

5. Write a compound sentence. [page 19]

   I disapprove of what you say, but I will defend to the death your right to say it. (Voltaire, French philosopher and writer, 1694–1778)

6. Write a complex sentence. [page 20]

   The finest thought runs the risk of being irretrievably forgotten if it is not written down. (Arthur Schopenhauer, German philosopher, 1788–1860)

7. Write a compound–complex sentence. [page 21]

   You may be disappointed if you fail, but you are doomed if you don't try. (Beverly Sills, U.S. opera singer, born 1929)

8. Write a sentence with an appositive. [page 78]

*Every great mistake has a halfway moment, **a split-second when it can be recalled and perhaps remedied.*** (Pearl S. Buck, U.S. writer, 1892–1973)

9. Write a sentence with a restrictive clause. [pages 80–81]

*People **who fly into a rage** always make a bad landing.*
(Will Rogers, U.S. humorist, 1879–1935)

10. Write a sentence with a non-restrictive clause. [pages 80–81]

*Turkey vultures, **which cruise hundreds of feet above the dense rain forests**, smell food on the forest floor.*

11. Begin a sentence with a prepositional phrase. [pages 10–12]

***For children**, leaf fall is just one of the odder figments of Nature, like hailstones or snowflakes. (A Natural History of the Senses* by Diane Ackerman, U.S. writer, b. 1948)

12. Begin a sentence with an adverb. [pages 9–10]

***Sideways,** spinning, the sled hit a bump in the hill and Jonas was jarred loose and thrown violently into the air. (The Giver* by Lois Lowry, U.S. writer, b. 1937)

13. Begin a sentence with an adjective followed by a verb.

*How **thin** and **sharp** and ghostly **white**
Is the slim curved **crook** of the moon tonight.*
(Langston Hughes, U.S. writer, 1902–1967)

14. Begin a sentence with a direct object. [pages 29–29]

***Courage** had she for the task that was before her.*

15. Use a present infinitive as a subject. [page 38]

***To lose patience** is to lose the battle.* (Mohandas K. Gandhi, Indian spiritual and political leader, 1869–1948)

16. Use a perfect infinitive as a subject.

   To have become a deeper man *is the privilege of those who have suffered.* (Oscar Wilde, Irish writer, 1854–1900)

17. Begin a sentence with a participle (an *-ing* word used as an adjective).

   Grunting, hissing, *a dozen buses pulled up behind me and threw open their doors.* (*High Tide in Tucson* by Barbara Kingsolver, U.S. writer, b. 1955)

18. Use a gerund (an *-ing* word used as a noun).

   Stumbling *is the fruit of haste.* (Jane Austen, English writer, 1775–1817).

19. Use a noun clause, in this case used as a direct object.

   Whose woods these are*, I think I know.* (Robert Frost, U.S. poet, 1874–1963)

20. Write a periodic sentence, which builds suspense by delaying the independent clause to the end.

   As far as the eye could see, all around, wherever I looked, snow was lifting and spiraling from the steppe. (*The Endless Steppe* by Esther Hautzig, Polish-born U.S. writer, b. 1930)

21. Write a simile, a comparison that uses the word *like* or *as*.

   Hating people is like burning down your own house to get rid of a rat. (Harry Emerson Fosdick, U.S. preacher and author, 1878–1969)

22. Write a metaphor, a comparison that says one thing *is* another.

   Service is the rent that you pay for room on this earth. (Shirley Chisolm, U.S. politician, b. 1924)

APPENDICES:
TIPS FOR SUCCESS IN SCHOOL

HOMEWORK

The following suggestions will help you to be successful with your homework.

1. 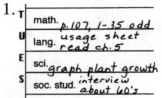 Write down each **assignment**. It's helpful to have an assignment notebook for this purpose and to write each assignment *on the day it is due*. That will help you as you plan your time and decide what you should work on first.

2. Be sure to take home all the **materials**—textbooks, notebooks, tools, etc.—that you'll need to complete your assignments.

3. Have a particular **place** where you regularly do your homework. This place should be well lit and should be equipped with any supplies you might need, such as a dictionary, thesaurus, and pencil sharpener. Your study area should also be free of distractions, especially television.

4.  As much as possible, do your homework at the same **time** each day. Find out what works best for you. Do you work most efficiently if you do your homework right after school, or do you work better if you have a break first? Do you work better if you have a large block of time, or do you need frequent breaks, even of a few minutes? Is it better for you to do your hardest subject first when you're fresh or to save it for last when you can give it your full attention? People will have different answers to these questions.

5. **Review** your notes each evening. If anything is unclear, check it yourself or ask your teacher or one of your classmates about it. This will make test preparation much easier for you.

6. **Practice** oral presentations in front of a mirror and then in front of a live audience. A few people are best, but a pet is better than no one.

CLASS PARTICIPATION

Participating wholeheartedly in class will help you to learn more efficiently. Then you'll have to spend less time doing homework.

1. Arrive at class prepared. That means that your homework is finished, you have all materials you need, and you are mentally prepared for the class activity. You'll feel confident and will be able to add to your knowledge of the subject.

2. Notice what the focus of the lesson is, and work toward the class's group goal. If the class is talking about the Louisiana Purchase, for example, don't bring up for discussion a souvenir that you bought during Mardi Gras in New Orleans.

3. Think about how today's lesson relates to other lessons you've had in this class recently—or to lessons you *will* have, if you know what they are.

4. Be involved in class. Give the activity or the discussion your full attention. Remember, however, that your involvement shouldn't interfere with the involvement of your classmates. Participation in discussion, for example, involves *listening* as well as speaking.

5. If oral participation is difficult for you, set a goal of participating once or twice each class. Then force yourself to do it. It's fine to answer questions even if you're not sure of the answer. You may find that you're right more often than you expect to be, and even if you're wrong, you'll probably learn something. At any rate, participation will get easier as you do more of it.

6. Be sure to ask a classmate or your teacher about anything that is unclear, either content being studied or requirements of an assignment. If you ask a classmate, choose someone who is informed.

TEST PREPARATION

1. Be totally involved in each class, and complete all assignments promptly and carefully.

2. Be sure to keep all notes and handouts in order. A looseleaf binder with dividers labeled for each subject generally works well.

3. Look over your notes each evening (even before a test is announced). Get clarification of anything you don't understand.

4. If there are things you need to memorize, such as capitals, dates, or vocabulary, begin as soon as the assignment is made. Divide the task into parts, memorizing some items each day.

5. Pay careful attention to any information your teacher gives you about the test. Be sure you know what material is to be covered and what type of question will be asked. Each type of question—matching, true-false, completion, or essay—requires slightly different preparation.

6. Begin studying for the test as soon as it is announced. Don't wait until the night before.

7. Complete any review sheets the teacher gives you. Do as much as possible without your textbook or notes; then check your answers.

8. Write down some questions that you think will be on the test. Exchange questions with a classmate for some test-taking practice.

9. If the test will have any essay questions, practice writing an essay answer. The teacher might give you an essay question ahead of time so that you can prepare a good response. Even if the teacher doesn't tell you, you might be able to guess what the teacher will ask you to write about. What did the teacher seem to consider important as you studied the chapter? Jot down some notes so that you can present complete information in an organized way. Be sure to put material into your own words. Check your facts. Edit your essay according to the guidelines on pages 135–136. If you needed to refer to your textbook or notes often while writing your essay, repeat this exercise until you can write independently.

10. Sometimes it works well to have a parent, sibling, or classmate quiz you over the material to be covered on the test. If this isn't convenient—or if you want to study more independently—prepare note cards or a two-column study sheet so that you can quiz yourself. If you're studying definitions, for example, write the word on one side of a note card and the definition on the other side. Or write the word in a left-hand column and the definition to the right. You'll then be able to cover half the material, quiz yourself, and check to see if you're right. Many types of factual material can be studied in this way.

11. Get a good night's sleep, and eat a good breakfast.

TEST TAKING

If you have been involved in class and have been doing your home-work, a test is an opportunity to show what you've learned and to find out what you still need to study.

1. Take time to read the directions. No matter how well you know the material, if you do the wrong thing, you might get a very low score.

2. Budget your time. If you're stuck on one item, don't waste too much time on it. Instead go on to other items, and go back to the difficult one later.

3. Read test questions carefully. The word *not*, for example, totally changes the meaning of a sentence.

4. See if the test itself can help you with troublesome items. For example, if you have to list fifteen prepositions and you can think of only twelve, maybe you can recognize some on the test.

5. When you have completed your test, take time to recheck your answers. Don't just *reread* the test, *rethink* it.

6. When you get your graded test back, be sure to gain an under-standing of items you missed. Consider whether you should do anything differently in preparing for or taking the next test.

ADDITIONAL RESOURCES

These are just a few favorites of the many excellent resources available. You'll find more listed on the GrammarAndMore website.

From Portico Books, publisher of *Hands-On English*

    The Activity Book (practice pages to aid mastery of concepts presented in this book)

    Hands-On Sentences (a card game that gives practice with parts of speech and sentence construction)

    Hands-On Icons (cards that make grammar visual and kinesthetic)

    Acu-Write and *LinguaPhile* (**Free** e-mail newsletters)

    "Make Your Voice Heard: Express Your Ideas Effectively" (**Free** online writing class)

Get more information about these products from the order form at the back of this book or from **www.GrammarAndMore.com**

Books from Other Publishers

    Asher, Sandy. *Where Do You Get Your Ideas? Helping Young Writers Begin*.

    Cassedy, Sylvia. *In Your Own Words: A Beginner's Guide to Writing*.

    Heiligman, Deborah. *The New York Public Library Kid's Guide to Research*.

    Heller, Ruth. **World of Language** series (small, colorful books that bring the parts of speech to life; *Kites Sail High: A Book About Verbs* is one title).

    Henderson, Kathy. *Market Guide for Young Writers: Where and How to Sell What You Write*.

    Janeczko, Paul B. *How to Write Poetry*.

    Lederer, Richard. *Pun and Games: Jokes, Riddles, Daffynitions, Tairy Fales, Rhymes, and More Word Play for Kids*.

    Levine, Dr. Mel. *Keeping A Head in School: A Student's Book About Learning Abilities and Learning Disorders*.

Websites

    Biography Maker (step-by-step process for converting facts to a lively story). www.bham.wednet.edu/bio/biomak2.htm

    Books from the Heart (kits for making hand-bound books and other keepsakes). www.BooksFromTheHeart.com

    Kid News (guidelines for writing various genres and an opportunity to publish on the Internet) www.kidnews.com

    Print Periodicals that Publish Children's Writing (includes addresses and type of material published) http://www.springfield.k12.il.us/resources/languagearts/readingwriting/Publish/periodicpubl.htm

    Research Papers (help in selecting a topic and beginning online research) www.researchpaper.com

    Writing Prompts (hundreds of ideas) www.canteach.ca/elementary/prompts.html

    Writing Successful College Admission Essays. www.sru.edu/depts/admissio/lagnese/essays.htm

SOUNDS REPRESENTED BY LETTERS

Although this page doesn't include every possibility, it will help you know the sounds that letters are likely to represent.

Vowels

a	**c**at, **a**corn, **a**te, **a**lone
ai, ay	m**ai**d, s**ay**
au, aw	**au**tumn, s**aw**
e	**e**nd, b**e**, th**e**se, lab**e**l
ee, ey	fr**ee**, k**ey**
ea	**ea**t, br**ea**d, st**ea**k
eu	f**eu**d, d**eu**ce
ew	f**ew**, gr**ew**
ei	c**ei**ling, v**ei**n
eigh	**eigh**t
i	**i**t, h**i**, f**i**nd, f**i**ne, penc**i**l, champ**i**on, mill**i**on,
ie	t**ie**, p**ie**ce
igh	s**igh**
o	**o**dd, g**o**, h**o**pe, c**o**ld, lem**o**n
oa, oe	c**oa**t, t**oe**
ow	sn**ow**, c**ow**
ou	**ou**t, s**ou**p
oo	sch**oo**l, b**oo**k
oi, oy	**oi**l, b**oy**
u	**u**p, p**u**pil, **u**se, fl**u**, circ**u**s
ue	bl**ue**, c**ue**
ui	s**ui**t

R-Controlled Vowels

ar	c**ar**, begg**ar**, w**ar**n
or	**or**, doct**or**, w**or**m
er, ir, ur	h**er**, b**ir**d, b**ur**n

Consonants

c	**c**at (generally /k/ before *a, o, u,* or a consonant)
	city (generally /s/ before *e, i,* or *y*)
g	**g**o (generally /g/ before *a, o, u,* or a consonant)
	gel (generally /j/ before *e, i,* or *y*)
q	**qu**een, cli**que** /k/
s	**s**o, bug**s**, wi**s**e
x	bo**x**, **x**ylophone
y	**y**ellow, m**y**, t**y**pe, bab**y**, repl**y**, g**y**m

Digraphs

ch	**ch**in, **ch**orus
th	**th**in, **th**is

Other Letter Combinations

tion	ac**tion**
sion	mis**sion**, vi**sion** /zhun/
ti	pa**ti**ent /sh/
ci	so**ci**al /sh/
tu	pic**tu**re /ch/

INDEX

Numbers in parentheses indicate a numbered item on the page listed.

179

181